S. F. Austin

GIANTS
of the
OLD WEST

By

FREDERICK R. *itchie* BECHDOLT

Essay Index Reprint Series

 BOOKS FOR LIBRARIES PRESS
FREEPORT, NEW YORK

STANDARD BOOK NUMBER:
8369-1020-6

LIBRARY OF CONGRESS CATALOG CARD NUMBER:
73-80382

To
BONNIE

ACKNOWLEDGMENT

The following is a partial list of the authorities to which the writer is indebted:

"American Fur Trade of the Far West," by H. M. Chittenden; "Ashley-Smith Explorations," by H. C. Dale; "Astoria," by Washington Irving; "Illinois-Missouri Gazetteer"; "Life of Stephen F. Austin," by E. C. Barker; "Border Wars of Texas," by J. T. de Shields; "History of Texas," by Henderson Yoakum; "History of Texas," by J. H. Brown; "Pictorial History of Texas," by Thrall; "North American States and Texas," by H. H. Bancroft; "Conquest of the Southwest," by Cyrus Townsend Brady; "Sam Houston, and the War of Independence in Texas," by A. M. Williams; "Autobiography of David Crockett" (Introduction by Hamlin Garland); "Justice of The Mexican War," by C. H. Owen; "The Quarterly of the Texas State Historical Association"; "The Fall of the Alamo," by R. M. Potter (Old South Leaflets); "American History Magazine"; "Texas Almanac" (1860) "Southwestern Historical Quarterly"; "History and Legends of the Alamo," by Adina de Zavala; "Magazine of American History" (1878); "Fraser's Magazine"; "Munsey's Magazine"; "Encyclopedia of the History of Missouri," edited by H. L. Conrad; "National Cyclopedia of American Biography"; "The Overland Pony Express," by Greene Majors; "Deseret News"; "The Martin Handcart Company," by Elder Andrew Jensen (from "Deseret News"); "Pioneers in the West, 1846 to 1878," by W. M. Egan; "The Trans-Mississippi West from 1803 to 1853," by Cardinal Goodwin; "Early Western Travels," edited by R. G. Thwaites (Pattie's personal narrative); "Commerce of the Prairies," by Josiah Gregg; "John A. Sutter's Journal" (copy of original in Bancroft Library); "Pioneer Days in the Southwest," by Charles Goodnight and others; "A History of California," by R. G. Cleland; "Oregon Trail," by Francis Parkman.

CONTENTS

ILLUSTRATIONS

MAPS

GIANTS OF THE OLD WEST

GIANTS OF THE OLD WEST

JOHN COLTER

THIS man John Colter was the first of a brave company. Intrepid souls, drawn by the love of high adventure, they struck out beyond the Mississippi toward the setting sun.

Trappers in buckskin, with their long-barreled rifles across their saddle bows; Texas colonists in homespun; dust-stained teamsters on the trail to distant Santa Fé; Mormon emigrants singing hymns as they pushed their two-wheeled hand-carts up the Platte Valley; gold-seekers toiling to break trails through the deep snows of the Sierra passes; stage-drivers and shotgun guards fighting off the Indians from the seats of the lurching Concords; hide-hunters wiping out the bison herds with their big-caliber Sharp's rifles; cowboys driving the wild longhorns northward from

3

the Rio Grande to the Yellowstone A mighty pageant in the blood and dust.

Bold men and their uncomplaining women; they made the conquest of the West. They went from peaceful eastern valleys, where life was safe and living easy, to find new homes, to make their fortunes, to get big wages—self-betterment was always the excuse. But with every one of them the underlying motive was the eagerness for high adventure, the willingness to take a chance against the Great Unknown. So, with serene indifference to what hazards lay ahead, they risked their dollars and they risked their lives. And to-day we travel in swift luxury along trails lined by the unmarked graves of their forgotten dead. The splendor of large cities has erased the hills and gullies from old camp grounds where men-folk died in battle and their women died in childbirth. All that is left of them is the story of the things they did. In the traditions of the nations none is more worth cherishing.

John Colter was a six-foot Virginian, wide-shouldered, lean of frame, wearing a fringed hunting-shirt of smoke-tanned buckskin, carrying a long-barreled flint-lock rifle over the crook of his arm. When he was a boy the itch for high adventure had brought him across the Alleghenies to fight the hostile Indians during the last years of the Revolutionary War. When peace came and settlers began to flock into the long Ohio Valley, the old desire returned—to wander beyond the smell of other men's camp-fires, to take a long chance against the Great Unknown.

Beyond the Mississippi untrodden wilds reached to the Shining Mountains. Beyond those snow-clad summits, which we call the Rockies now, the Great Unknown stretched to the shores of the Pacific Ocean. In that summer of 1803, when men of middle age were yarning of Lexington and Valley Forge on drowsy tavern porches, President Thomas Jefferson—uneasy under a longing like that of John Colter—was outfitting an expedition to explore this *terra incognita* and plant the Stars and Stripes beside the western sea.

So it came that Captain Meriwether Lewis and Lieutenant William Clark took their little company of enlisted men down the Ohio River late that summer. And among the volunteers who manned the sweeps on the clumsy flatboats was John Colter. They wintered near the river's mouth. In May the little village of St. Louis—but newly come into this nation—saw them depart, in two pirogues and a bateau, up the Mississippi for the unknown Northwest. They entered the muddy, snag-strewn Missouri. They passed the last settlement. The wilderness swallowed them.

More than two years went by. Summer was on the wane; the wild grapes were turning purple in the thickets along the river banks, when they came forth again to tell the world how they had followed the Missouri to its source; how they had crossed the Rockies and traversed the dusty sage-brush plains along the Snake; how they had descended the Columbia to plant their country's flag where the gray swells of the Pacific swept the lonely sands of Oregon.

Of that company that had departed, two were lacking. One was a soldier who had died of sickness where Sioux City stands to-day; there is a monument of rock to mark his grave. The other was John Colter, for whom no monument was ever raised. The lure of high adventure had been too much for him again and he had remained in the wilderness.

A solitary horseman, clad in buckskin, with his long-barreled rifle across his thighs and a bunch of beaver traps clanking against the withers of his Indian pony, wandering along the sage-brush hills beside the distant Yellowstone. The first of that long procession of adventurers who passed beyond the Mississippi, onward toward the setting sun, to take the West and hold it. With all the men and the uncomplaining women in the blood and dust of that mighty pageant there was a common motive: the eagerness to take a chance against the Great Unknown. But in every case there was a more immediate excuse for faring forth—the hope of bettering themselves. They risked their dollars and their lives to make their fortunes or to get new homes. With John Colter the bait was furs. He stayed to trap the beaver. When the thaws of springtime came and the first wild geese were honking northward, he built himself a log canoe; he started down the river with his bales of pelts.

He reached the muddy Missouri; he slipped down through the prairies of the wild Assiniboines and Mandans, past the mud-hut villages of the fierce Arickarees; past Council

Bluffs, where Lewis and Clark had smoked the peace pipe with the chiefs of six tribes nearly three years before. Not far from the Platte's mouth he heard the sound of singing. He saw a file of voyageurs upon the bank, bedecked in scarlet sashes and bright handkerchiefs, bending their backs to a long towrope. A clumsy craft—somewhat like a canalboat, somewhat like the old ark of which the Bible tells us—came into sight around a bend. The singing stopped; the cordelle slackened to the stubby mast; the keel-boat swung in to shore. John Colter paddled his canoe alongside.

He heard his name called. Those were familiar voices. Among the crowd of swarthy half-breed *courriers des bois* who were lounging on the roof of the cargo house he saw two white men whom he knew—George Drouillard and John Potts, who had crossed the continent with the Lewis and Clark expedition. But another voice was addressing him and he turned his eyes from these companions to a thickset man who was looking down upon him from the runway beside the cargo house. Shrewd eyes of black, dark features wherein strength and nobility were mingled; a crispness of speech that went well with the Spanish accent. It was Manuel Lisa, most restless and most daring of the early traders, on his way up-river with an expedition to the Shining Mountains.

The easy-natured voyageurs rested on the bank; the swarthy *courriers des bois,* in their moccasins and beaded buckskins, smoked on the cargo house, while the first of the free trappers and the first of the Rocky Mountain fur-traders talked on the deck. An hour went by. Manuel Lisa waved his hand and shouted a command. The voyageurs bent to their toil; the cordelle tightened to the masthead as their old French Canadian chanson sounded clear. The keel-boat moved on against the tawny current. And with it went John Colter, returning to the wilderness again.

The dreary gales of springtime passed. They reached the mouth of the Yellowstone —the parting of the ways. The main stream led into the country of the sullen Blackfeet, the tributary to the country of the Crows. Fur-trading in those days was a rough game, and none played it more roughly than the bleak-faced Scotsmen of the great northwestern company with whom the Blackfeet trafficked at Fort Edmonton. John Colter had seen enough on the Lewis and Clark expedi- tion to know the chances that Lisa's men would run of leaving their scalps to dry on the lodge- poles of these northern Indians if they fol- lowed the Missouri.

"Build your first post in the country of the Crows," was the advice of the Virginian. "I'll find their villages and smoke the pipe of peace with them. Later on, you can send some one to make a big talk to the Blackfeet."

So Lisa bought ponies from a band of As- siniboines, who had come to massacre the white men and had remained to trade. And the company went up the valley of the Yel- lowstone, with John Colter riding in the lead. On the sweep of sage-brush upland where the Bighorn finds its mouth they cached their goods; the Creole voyageurs and *engagés* went to work down in the river bottom, cutting logs for a stockade. And John Colter saddled his pony to set forth in search of the wander- ing Absorakees, whom we white men have miscalled the Crows.

Southward he rode among the wide drab hills. A solitary figure in a lonely land. About his brow a red handkerchief binding his lank·

locks; a powder-horn slung over his shoulder;
in his belt a knife with buckhorn handle; leggings and loose hunting-shirt of smoke-tanned
buckskin fringed with the long quills of the
porcupine; behind the cantle of his rawhide
saddle a buffalo robe, rolled round his small
store of salt and powder and gaudy trinkets
for the savages; across his lap the long-
barreled rifle with which he was to get his
food.

Day after day. On up the valley of the Bighorn. Long rides and lonely camps beneath
the stars. Southward into the gray Wyoming
hills. Off to the left the range which bears
the river's name rose to the snow-clad summit
of Cloud Peak. He passed the mouth of the
Shoshone, the mouth of the Graybull. He
saw the blue wall of the main divide, with its
line of snow peaks in the west. He traveled
by the deep gorge above whose upper end the
stream is called Wind River. He swung into
the west. Among the clumps of sage the
travois-trails grew fresher. One evening,
somewhere north of where the town of Lan-
der stands to-day, he saw the pointed lodges
of the Crow village on a stretch of level grass-
land by a little stream. With his right hand

raised, palm forward, far above his head, he rode toward the group of warriors who came forth to meet him.

That night a little fire burned in the largest of the lodges. Around the wavering flame a circle of dark faces; faces of old men, seamed deeply, framed with braids of snow-white hair; faces of grave chiefs, under the huge war-bonnets whose eagle plumes rustled faintly to every movement; faces of medicine men, with craft written in every line; faces of young warriors with cruel lips and little eager red flecks dancing in their black eyes. In the midst of them John Colter.

He was making his big talk.

More than two hundred miles from any white man. Those who listened lived by theft and war. As suspicious—and almost as lawless in their actions—as the wild animals which they hunted; they understood no word of his language; he knew perhaps a half-dozen words of theirs. If he could convince them by this sadly handicapped oration, they would take a chance and bring their furs to the white men, of whom they knew only by far-fetched rumor. If he could not convince them, his scalp was going to remain down here in the Absorakee country, possibly as an adornment to this same lodge where he was sitting now. So he did the best he could, for the most part in the sign language, to tell them of the great white trader who had come from the lands of the rising sun to be their friend and bring them goods for their furs. When he had done he gave them presents from his buffalo robe. The red-bowled pipe of peace, with dyed eagle plumes dangling from its yard-long stem, went round.

The talk had succeeded. So well, in fact, that the peace which began that night down in the Wind River country was never broken by the Crows. And that is more perhaps than can be said for any peace the white men made in the early days with any other tribe of Indians.

There was another village of their people, the chiefs told Colter, somewhere in the West, and if he stayed they would take him thither. So he went with them over the Wind River mountains by Union Pass, and for the second time he saw the waters which ran to the Pacific. They followed the Gros Ventre River, with the Three Tetons standing out against the sky before them; they traveled through

Jackson's Hole and over the Teton Pass. They found the Crow village in the level basin north of the place where Victor, Idaho, stands to-day.

One day while Colter was sojourning with these people a swarm of Gros Ventres swooped down upon the lodges. The battle lasted until evening, and when the Gros Ventres finally retired they laid their defeat to the white man whose long-barreled rifle emptied a saddle every time it spoke. They brought the story to their allies the Blackfeet and in good time it bore its fruit.

· On the morning after that battle the Crows departed by Teton Pass for their own country. But Colter, with the ragged hole left by a Gros Ventre arrow in his thigh, decided to take a short cut, of which they had told him, to the mouth of the Bighorn. So he journeyed alone across the rugged pass just north of the Three Tetons, past Jackson's Lake, over the Divide whose dense forests of lodge-pole pine separate the headwaters of the Snake and the Yellowstone. There he came down to mighty geysers hurling their steaming floods skyward with a noise like thunder, to boiling springs of many colors on the shores of a mountain lake, to cliffs of black glass and to the canyon whose lofty walls, more brilliantly tinted than the rainbow, pen in the great falls of the river. And when in after-years he told the story of these wonders of the Yellowstone National Park, men said he was a liar.

Autumn was drawing near by the time he reached the stockaded walls of the trading-post, and Lisa was preparing for his down-river journey to St. Louis with the season's harvest of beaver skins. John Colter gave him the news of the peace with the Crows, and the trader departed, eager for the coming of the next spring, when he would return with goods to sell the savages for furs. Before he went it was agreed that the Virginian should journey to the Three Forks of the Missouri when the first warm weather came, to try his luck as an envoy to the warlike Blackfeet.

Winter came down upon the land. Within the log stockade the *engagés* and lowly "pork eaters" went about their daily drudgery. The jovial voyageurs gathered in the close, hot bunk-rooms, telling weird stories of the loup-garou in the dark Canadian forests, of pallid ghosts and miracles in the little settlements north of Sault Ste. Marie, singing the long boat songs which their grandfathers had sung on the St. Lawrence. The swarthy half-breed *courriers des bois* lounged in silence on the outskirts of the noisy groups. John Colter and a half-dozen others of his kind kept to themselves. In that little coterie of lean-framed, leathern-faced Americans there were George Drouillard and John Potts, who had been with Lewis and Clark; Edward Robinson, who always wore a colored handkerchief above his fringe of grizzled hair to conceal the hideous scar where Kentucky Indians had torn away his scalp; Jacob Rezner and John Hoback. They talked of beaver dams, of roving Indians and mountain passes; they listened while the tall Virginian described his summer's wanderings; they scanned the maps which he scratched with a sharp stick upon the earthen floor.

The springtime came. John Colter took Potts with him and departed for the Three Forks of the Missouri, not far from where the town of Bozeman, Montana, stands today. To trap the beaver and to wait the coming of the Blackfeet Indians from their winter camping grounds; that was the idea. Then, when the savages arrived, Colter would go to their village, with his hand uplifted in the peace signal—to make his talk with the chiefs and the old men.

A hazardous project at the best, for the canny Scotchmen of the Northwest Fur Company had inflamed these Blackfeet with suspicion against the American traders. At that it might have succeeded if it had not been for two things. One of these was the tale which the Gros Ventres had brought back from that day-long battle in the Teton Basin to these, their cousins—the story of the white man who had helped their ancient enemies, the Crows. The other circumstance was due to blind luck, by which the meeting—to put it mildly —was unpropitious.

It happened on a morning when the spring was drawing on toward summer. Since the crack of day, Colter and Potts had been visiting their line of traps. The sun was well up and they were coming down the stream—it was a broad creek which ran into the Jefferson—in their log canoe. Of a sudden they heard, ahead of them and on both sides, the tramp of many hoofs, the cracking of the dense willow brush.

"Indians," Colter whispered, and backed

water with his paddle. But Potts maintained it was a herd of buffalo and taunted him with being a coward. While they were arguing, the bushes parted on the nearer bank; they saw dark faces peering out at them. The time for flight was gone now; there was only one thing to do and Colter did it. He headed for the bank.

The willows thicket was full of those dark forms. The bow touched the bank. A score of savage faces looked down upon the white men. Potts stood up between the thwarts, his rifle in his hand. A strapping warrior leaped into the water; he tore the weapon from the trapper's grasp. Colter sprang from the canoe. He wrenched the rifle away from its captor and handed it back to Potts.

There passed an instant during which the situation hung in the balance, where the Virginian's boldness had placed it. But panic had the best of Potts and he shoved off. A bow-string twanged.

"I'm wounded, Colter," he called from the middle of the stream.

"Come back," the other bade him. "It's your only chance." Even then, perhaps, he could have braved the thing out and bluffed his way to make his big talk with the chiefs. But Potts flung the rifle to his shoulder and fired at the warrior who had shot that arrow. Before the smoke had cleared away from the muzzle, he sank down in the bottom of the canoe with more than twenty feathered shafts in his body.

A dozen savages seized Colter. Knives yearned toward his throat; the points of feathered lances pricked his skin. He stood there on the bank where they had dragged him, unmoved so far as they could see. He knew that was his only chance to live. They led him forth out of the willow thickets upon the sage-brush flat. They stripped his clothes from him until he was as naked as on the day he was born.

According to their idea of a good time, they proposed to have some fun with him before he died.

The chief of the village was acting as the master of the revels. He lined up the warriors on a mark. Save for their moccasins and the shreds of loin cloth, they were as naked as the captive. In his right hand every member of that long line bore a single weapon, according to his choice in such matters—

lance, hatchet, stone-headed war-club or knife. Firearms and bows were barred.

"Is the white man a good runner?" the chief asked. Colter, who had a pretty good idea of what these preparations tended toward, shook his head. He explained, to the very best of his ability, that he was slow of foot. Which was a lie, as any one who knew him could have told the chief.

His back was toward the willow thickets of the creek. Before him the flat stretched for six miles—sage-brush and prickly-pear and not a single tree—to the timbered bottom of the Jefferson Fork. On the strength of that lie the chief took him three hundred yards ahead of the line of warriors.

"If you wish to live," he told Colter, "save yourself." As he spoke, the shrill war-whoop rose from one end of that line behind him to the other. The Virginian leaped forward. The race was on.

Six miles ahead the timber showed, a low dark streak against the pallid sage-brush. His refuge—provided he could gain it.

He ran until his heart was pounding and the blood was roaring in his ears. Now he had gone a mile; now two; the number of pursurers was growing smaller. The war-whoop was no longer sounding. They needed all the breath they had for this stubborn chase. Now he had gone three miles and he could no longer hear the sound of their feet; he looked behind; only a handful of them left and they were far away—save one who was hanging on within two hundred yards. Four miles; the timber along the river was showing plainly; he could almost make out some of the separate trees. The single warrior had begun to gain.

During the next mile the blood gushed from Colter's mouth and nose, smearing his chest with a sticky patch of red. And when he looked behind again the solitary Blackfoot was not more than fifty feet away. The Virginian took five or six more strides; then whirled with hands upraised. The startled savage hurled his lance, and as it left his hand he fell. The weapon buried its head in the sand between the two and broke off half-way down the shaft. Before the warrior could pick himself up, Colter sprang upon the spear; he tore it forth and plunged it through the Indian's body. Then he turned and staggered on across the last mile into the shelter of the timber.

Out in the middle of the stream there was a sand-bar, and at the head of this little island a huge raft of driftwood which had come down with the spring floods. He swam out to the jam and dived beneath it. Where several of the entangled logs formed a roof above the water he raised his head. Here he remained, neck deep in the icy current, while the whooping Blackfeet swarmed over the raft. The morning was still young. They kept up the hunt until the afternoon was growing late. At last they withdrew; and when the darkness came, John Colter swam downstream, to crawl at last, half-frozen, to the bank.

It was one hundred and fifty miles from the trading-post. Stark naked and weaponless, he started on the journey, with the stars to guide him. Sage-brush and prickly-pear; sharp rocks on the ridges to gash his bleeding feet. For food he found some roots. And at the end of the seventh day he staggered into the log stockade at the mouth of the Bighorn, to tell the story of his great ordeal.

That autumn and during the next year John Colter continued to go forth from Lisa's fort, to get the beaver, to sell the skins to the trader who had given him his traps and his supplies. Then, in the spring, he went down river to St. Louis, where he described his wanderings to William Clark, now at the head of Indian affairs in the West. And Clark added new places to the map which he and Meriwether Lewis had made of the Rocky Mountain wilderness.

Nor was that all. On La Charette Creek, where he married and built himself a home near old Daniel Boone, Colter was visited by men with John Jacob Astor's land expedition, whose object was to found a trading-post at the mouth of the Columbia. He told them of the Union and the Teton passes, by which, in months to come, they made their way across the Rockies instead of taking the longer northern route which Lewis and Clark had used.

And in the future still greater results were to come from this man's exploits. Manuel Lisa and his partner, Andrew Henry, built a log fort up in the Blackfoot country; but the feud which had begun with Colter still endured. The Indians drove out the trappers.

George Drouillard died fighting in a day-
long battle, with his dead pony for a breast-
work, not far from the spot where the Virginian had undergone his great ordeal. The Gros
Ventres slew old Robinson, John Hoback and
Jacob Rezner at the headwaters of the Snake
across the mountains. The American traders
retired from the country of the Crows. And,
years later, by the guidance of these Absorakees—who still maintained the peace which
John Colter had made with them—the trappers of a younger generation found the great
natural highway across the wilderness to California and Oregon.

ASHLEY AND HIS YOUNG MEN

IT was in the days following the War of 1812. A period of restlessness, when many eyes were turned toward the West. Huge canvas-covered wagons were lumbering across the Alleghenies, laden with household goods; whole fleets of flatboats were floating down the Ohio and the Mississippi, carrying settlers into the wilderness. Land colonies were being formed; filibustering expeditions were outfitting; speculators were making their fortunes; booms were collapsing. An era when riches and ruin went hand in hand; but to the ruin none paid heed.

Of the times William Ashley was a typical product. Somewhere about forty. Handsome in a ruddy way, with highly polished boots and a gold-headed cane; starched ruffles on his shirt; skin-tight breeches and a wide-skirted coat; a high-topped beaver hat with a rolling brim. He lived just outside the growing town of St. Louis in a large house with green shutters and long verandas; but home did not see him very often at the time when this story begins; he had too many irons in the fire.

Politics kept him busy; he was lieutenant-governor of Missouri; and he hoped to be governor some day. He was general of the state militia, and he liked the title as well as he did the showy uniform. He was interested in two or three banks, but he kept his money so busy working for him that when he wanted capital for a new project he usually had to borrow. One of that adventurous breed who are at their best in business when they are on the aggressive, who utterly lack the cautious instinct. A breed which was to do great things during the next half-century beyond the Mississippi.

Men used to do much of their traveling on horseback in those days. Perhaps, in your mind's eye, you can see William Ashley— top-hat and all—riding down the rutted road across green prairie stretches and through patches of woodland, to the village of Potosi, more than fifty miles away. The chances are you have never heard of Potosi. And, if you depend on any history of these United States, the chances are you never will hear. Yet in this townlet—it was then of less than one thousand souls—were born two projects—commercial enterprises both of them—which changed this nation's destiny. Had it not been for them, our western boundary would now be the summit of the Rocky Mountains; Texas and the rest of the Southwest would be foreign territory. It was one of these projects that took William Ashley to Potosi.

Just then the village was dead. The lead mines were not working and the smelter had shut down. Lack of demand for metal following the war's end had brought the slump. Moses Austin and his son Stephen, who owned the smelter, had sold out. They had departed for the wild country west of Louisiana, where they had a concession from the Spaniards to found a colony. The story of their real-estate venture out of which came Texas and its consequences belongs elsewhere. But its conception has a bearing on this tale.

For it is something more than coincidence that the same itch which drove these two men toward the setting sun began to work on their associate with their departure. Politics had brought Ashley close to Stephen Austin, who had been a member of the state legislature; business had brought him closer, for he was

part owner of a lead mine whose metal came
to the smelter. And, now that the Austins had
gone, he too was figuring on a westward venture along with another of Potosi's leading
citizens.

This was Andrew Henry. A tall, quiet-
spoken man, somewhere near fifty, with gray
streaks in his dark hair. Ten years before, he
had been up the Missouri with Manuel Lisa,
the fur-trader, fighting Blackfeet Indians and
eating horse meat to keep from starving beyond the Rockies. Now he was a sedate liver,
a lover of books; he played the violin of evenings, one of those methodical bachelors who
do not want to be disturbed. But he had told
Ashley of those days in the fur country; and
Ashley came, on fire with the glowing visions,
to arouse the old restlessness which had been
sleeping for a decade.

To hire men and ascend the Missouri. To
penetrate the country of the upper river and
the country of the Rocky Mountains. To
pass the Rockies and to build trading-posts
throughout the wilderness beyond. Since the
War of 1812 the hostile Indians and the
British fur companies had held all this territory. So far as our Government was con-

cerned they could go on holding it. To fight
the savages and to outmaneuver the Hudson's
Bay factors, and to do these things without
aid from Washington. That was the idea of
the Rocky Mountain Fur Company, formed
by William H. Ashley and Andrew Henry in
this little village of Potosi, Missouri.

So, on the twentieth of March, 1822, there
appeared in the "Missouri Republican" a
want advertisement. It read:

To enterprising young men. The subscriber
wishes to engage one hundred young men to ascend the Missouri River to its source, there to
be employed for two or three years. For partic-
ulars inquire of Major Andrew Henry near the
lead mines in the county of Washington; or of the
subscriber near St. Louis. (Signed) William H.
Ashley.

The enterprising young men came; lank
youths in homespun from the backwoods
settlements, bull-necked boatmen who had
fought and roistered at every landing from
Pittsburgh to New Orleans, runaway appren-
tices; and with these members of a later generation, a sprinkling of grizzled fellows in
buckskin hunting-shirts, whose love of adven-

ture was the only young thing about them. On a spring morning all the town of St. Louis turned out to watch this company depart up-river in two keel-boats—ladies in flaring hoopskirts; merchants with their high beaver hats and strapped trousers; wealthy old French Creoles and their wives; and round the edges of the crowd a fringe of ragged negro slaves. A file of swarthy voyageurs from Michilimackinac at each of the tow-lines, decked out in gaudy kerchiefs and sashes, singing an old St. Lawrence boat song. The lines tightened; the clumsy boats went slowly out of sight.

On one of the cargo houses William Ashley sat beside his partner. All that he knew of this wilderness to which he was going was that it held large riches. But he was soon to learn more of its ways. They entered the Missouri and passed through thick forests where the deer came down to the banks and the wild pigeons broke the branches with their weight. They emerged into wide prairies and the spring gales howled down to meet them; the ugly current rushed at them like an enemy from ambush. One day near Fort Osage it caught the lead boat and swept it against a snag. Five minutes later the men were swimming for their lives; the boat and cargo were at the bottom of the river. Half of the goods and the equipment gone. All Ashley had and all he had been able to borrow were tied up in this expedition. The country of the beaver was still more than a thousand miles away.

The weeks went by. On the lonely prairies above the place where Bismarck stands to-day they parted with some of their goods to purchase ponies from the Mandans. A few days later, while half the men were herding the horses along the bank and the other half were on the boat, a huge war party of Assiniboines came whooping across the wide grasslands —and the newly bought ponies melted away before them like clouds before the wind. Nothing to do but halt and delve into the sadly diminished stock of goods to trade for more animals. Ashley did some figuring— and returned to St. Louis to try and borrow more money.

Henry went on. He took his men as far as the Great Falls of the Missouri. There the fierce Blackfeet stole upon them one morning and killed four men. They dogged the main body; they ambushed trapping parties. No day passed without a skirmish. In the end Henry turned back. He split his company into squads of three and four; they worked their way eastward, trapping through the Little Rockies and the Judith Basin. When winter came they built log cabins and holed up. With the coming of spring they went on to the mouth of the Yellowstone, where Henry and a few had gone ahead to build a fort.

A rough and ready crowd. Just to get an idea of them, take this incident—the first on record of those shooting affrays by which the law of right and wrong was enforced, without regard to printed statutes, in the old West. In the outfit were three men: Mike Fink, Carpenter and Talbot, close companions, and they wintered at the mouth of the Mussel-shell. Here Fink and Carpenter fell out over a squaw and did not speak to each other for months. But in the early spring, when they reached Henry's fort, they made it up again. At least, Carpenter did and Fink shook hands with him.

Here in the stockaded walls there was plenty of fiery whisky. All hands were drinking freely. And this Mike Fink—he was a burly man with a voice like a bull—proposed to Carpenter that they cement their truce by a little ceremony which they had often practised in the days of their old friendship. The two were faultless riflemen and this rite of theirs consisted in one standing with a tin cup full of whisky on his head while the other, at a distance of sixty paces, shot a hole in the mug. Now when Mike Fink made this proposition Carpenter agreed. But when the former won the toss for the first shot, there was something in his face which made Carpenter doubt the sincerity of his protested friendship. Being of a breed which did not back up, he went to the third of the trio, Talbot, to whom he told his suspicions.

"If he draws down too far," he added, "I leave you my rifle, powder-horn and pistol." Then he filled the cup with whisky and placed it on his head, while Mike Fink stepped off the customary distance. And a few moments later Carpenter's forebodings were justified; he lay with a bullet hole in the center of his forehead and Mike Fink loudly cursed his poor marksmanship. Talbot tucked the dead man's pistol under his hunting-shirt and said no word at all.

Nor did he speak about the matter later.

But he did hang close to Fink. Where the one was the other always went. And one day, when the red-hot trading whisky had the best of him, Fink made his boast that he had done that killing in cold blood. Talbot said nothing. But the old story goes that he was smiling when he drew Carpenter's pistol from beneath his hunting-shirt and shot the murderer between the eyes.

While these rough and ready men of his were waiting for him at the mouth of the Yellowstone, William Ashley was scouring northern Missouri for more money. The fact that he was already one hundred thousand dollars in debt at a time when banks were failing right and left did not appall him. The hazards which faced his venture up there in the wilderness did not break down his serene optimism. He went to men not only sure that he was going to repay them but that he was going to make them rich. And he got the money. In St. Louis that spring the "Missouri Republican" carried another want ad, to the same effect as the first one. Enterprising young men came to town hunting William Ashley. Among them were Jedediah Smith, who had carried his Bible with him all the way

from New York State; Jim Bridger, who
had slipped away from a blacksmith to whom
he was apprenticed; Etienne Provost—and
half a dozen other youths, whose names are
now printed on the western map. More than
one hundred in the company, including a
sprinkling of old-timers and a couple of dozen
French voyageurs. But the young fellows
were in the majority.

Up-river through the woods into the prairies, and on up. The voyageurs sang at the
long tow-lines; they sang, breasting the heavy
sweeps. Snags lay in ambush and the tawny
current strove to entrap them. But their luck
was with them—for the time. The spring
passed and it was on the night of the first of
June—they were at the mouth of the Cannon-
ball—when the wilderness showed its teeth
again to William Ashley.

A sultry night, and heat lightning was
flashing where the sky and prairie met. Always the distant *thud—thud—thud* of a war-
drum in the air. The two keel-boats were
moored close to the eastern bank. The voyageurs were snoring on the decks. On a sand-
bar which reached out from the western shore
forty or fifty of the men lay in their blankets,

in charge of a hundred horses which Ashley
had bought from the Indians that day. On the
summit of a low bluff overlooking them the
black shadows of a log stockade stood out
against the stars. It was the fort of the Arickarees, whose mud huts stood within. And that
never-ending war-drum was in their other village farther up the stream. While the night
was in its beginning, old Edward Rose had
come to Ashley and warned him to take those
men and horses away from the sand-bar; the
Rees, he said, were contemplating treachery.

A saturnine man, this Rose, half-Cherokee
and with a streak of negro; in days gone by
a Mississippi River pirate—some said a murderer. Ten years with the Crows and two years
with the Arickarees; and a squaw in each tribe.
Perhaps it was his hard name; at any rate,
Ashley did not take his advice.

The night went on and the first streaks of
dawn came in the east. Objects grew plainer
on the sand-bar. The logs in the stockade were
beginning to show. Suddenly, from the length
of the fort, thin flashes leaped through the
half-light; the shrill war-yell of the Rees
mingled with the cracking of their muskets.

Down by the water wounded men were

groaning; horses were scuffling, pulling back at their picket ropes; bewildered youths were shouting to one another as they rolled out of their blankets, to taste for the first time the unholy confusion of battle. And, on the sand among them, twelve dead men lay. Across the river Ashley was ordering the voyageurs to bring the keel-boats to the west bank; the swarthy French Canadians were in blind panic, and he might as well have tried to give orders to the current which was sweeping past. While he was cursing them some one cut the mooring lines and the clumsy boats began drifting down-stream.

Then two of the younger men on board took a skiff and rowed to the aid of their companions. Eight or ten horses were lying dead upon the sand-bar. Jedediah Smith, the youth who carried his Bible with him and said his prayers every night before rolling up in his blankets, was among the crowd, lying behind one of the carcasses, using his long-barreled rifle as coolly as Edward Rose, the former river pirate, who was on his belly near-by, seeking a target through the crannies in the stockade.

"Take off the wounded," the survivors bade

the pair in the skiff. They held their ground until the keel-boats were drifting out of reach; then struck out and swam for them. Fourteen killed and ten sorely wounded was the count; the keel-boats ten miles down-stream; the voyageurs in flat mutiny. And Andrew Henry waiting for them with his party at the mouth of the Yellowstone.

"Some one has got to take the news to Henry," Ashley said.

"I'll go." That was Jedediah Smith.

He went. Two hundred and fifty miles, the way he had to travel. The Indians out and the wilderness around him. Riding by night and hiding by day and getting his food with his rifle when he dared to use it. When Andrew Henry came down-river with his party, Ashley began to see that these enterprising young men who had answered his want ad were good stuff.

The weeks went by. It took the better part of the summer to join forces with the military and the Missouri fur company in a campaign against the Arickarees. Autumn was getting near when Andrew Henry took a selected number of the employees—in which the French Canadians were not included—and made his way overland up to the Yellowstone. More money. They had to have it. So Ashley went down-river to St. Louis to borrow it. It took a deal of courage to make the conquest of the lands beyond the Mississippi. But little has been said of the bravery of those men who risked their last cent, along with the money of those who trusted them—and threw in their own good names—to back these others, their companions in pioneering. This man Ashley was deep in debt. At a time when Missouri was just getting over a dozen staggering bank failures he had already succeeded in raising some fifty thousand dollars more. Now he was coming back, with bad news in place of beaver skins, to seek still further funds. One of less faith would have been looking for a job by which to mend his broken fortunes. But his faith was large and he stuck to his task. What is more, he got the money.

In the meantime, Andrew Henry and his party traveled with saddle ponies and pack animals into the Northwest. A weary road and dangerous. Talbot, who had slain his friend's murderer last spring, was swept from his horse and drowned crossing the Grand River. A few days farther on Hugh Glass, an old backwoodsman from Pennsylvania, was mangled by a grizzly-bear. They left two youths to care for him until he died; and, when these thought the breath was departing from his body, they abandoned him. But he was too tough a customer for death yet; he awoke from his coma and crawled, without so much as a hunting-knife, one hundred miles across the prairie on his hands and knees; for food he had some roots and berries, and a buffalo calf which he took away from a band of lobo wolves. He reached a trading-post on the Missouri and recovered, to make his way to the mouth of the Bighorn, where he found the rest of the company in winter quarters months later.

Edward Rose, the negroid half-breed who had warned Ashley against the Rees, was still with the expedition. Ten years among the Crows, a chief in the tribe, he was on his way to rejoin his adopted people. It was from this old renegade that young Jedediah Smith and Tom Fitzpatrick got certain information which brought large consequences. With the directions which the former river pirate gave them, the youthful Methodist and his companion took a small party southward from

the mouth of the Powder River into the country of the Crows. When they rejoined the
main body at the mouth of the Bighorn late
in the autumn they brought a story which the
Indians had told them, of a low pass across
the Rockies in the south and, beyond the summit, a country full of beaver dams.

This tale fired the ambition of the enterprising young men. In the springtime Jedediah Smith, Tom Fitzpatrick and Etienne
Provost took, each of them, a band of these
greenhorns. As free trappers—grubstaked by
the company to whom they were to sell what
furs they got—they departed to seek that pass.
Southward up the Bighorn, on from the Wind
River Valley to the Sweetwater, up the Sweetwater—and then they saw the mountains end-
ing like a promontory coming down into the
sea. They crossed the sage-brush uplands and
they found the waters running to the west.
Through that wide gateway, in days to come,
a nation was to travel to the western limit of
this continent.

But the destinies of nations were not bother-
ing these young fellows. They were after
beaver pelts. And the valley of Green River
into which they traveled was full of the ani-

mals. When a band of Gros Ventres stole the horses of Tom Fitzpatrick's company, the white men were too busy with their trapping to pursue them. They kept on gathering their harvest of furs until it was time to take their catch to the trading-post. Then they trailed the Gros Ventres to their village and stole back the horses with as many more as they could drive off in the night.

A busy summer. Young Jedediah Smith got as far west as the Snake River country before snow flew. Over there he ran across a band of Iroquois Indians under Alexander Ross of the Hudson's Bay Company. They had worked their way eastward from Fort Vancouver on the lower Columbia, and had nine hundred beaver skins. But the Snake River Indians had stolen their horses and they were out of food. In days gone by the predecessors of the Hudson's Bay had driven John Jacob Astor's men out of these regions. So now, when Jedediah Smith convoyed these half-starved wanderers to Pierre's Hole, near the Three Tetons, where help awaited them, his religious scruples did not prevent him from exacting the nine hundred beaver skins in payment.

During that autumn the bales of furs began to come down-river to St. Louis. And William Ashley began to suspect that the riches, of which he had been so serenely certain, were now at hand. It looked as if his days of importuning men for loans were coming to their end.

In the spring of 1825 Ashley went out to this new fur country which his young men had discovered. And when he went he traveled by a route which Tom Fitzpatrick had happened on in bringing beaver skins eastward during the previous autumn. Instead of going up the Missouri by boat, he journeyed horseback, with a pack train, up the valley of the Platte. And so the last link on the long road across the continent to Oregon was beaten down to a trail.

Instead of carrying their skins to the trading-post that year, the trappers met in a mountain meadow in the upper Green River country. Here came a multitude of friendly Indians, with pelts, to trade. Here Ashley learned how, last winter, young Jim Bridger had left the cabin on Bear River where he and three companions were holed up, and had followed down the stream to discover the

Great Salt Lake. And here came Johnson Gardner, another of the enterprising young men, with one hundred packs of beaver pelts —a fortune in itself—which he had gotten over in Cache Valley. Peter Skeen Ogden of the Hudson's Bay Company was the man for whom those furs were intended; but his half-breed employees were out of food and discontented—and Johnson Gardner had made the purchase for a song. That cache alone made William Ashley a rich man.

Henceforth, instead of seeking out the trading-posts, the trappers gathered, every summer, at an appointed spot in the mountains. To this place came the Indians. And hither the pack trains journeyed from St. Louis with the whisky and the trade goods. When the bartering was done and the whisky drunk, the white men and the Indians departed, to meet somewhere else next season. The days of the slow-moving river boats and the timid voyageurs were over; the days of the horseback rovers, with their long-barreled rifles and their rolls of bedding behind the saddles, had come.

Andrew Henry had already retired from the company. In 1826 Ashley sold out to

Smith, Jackson and Sublette. He had succeeded—it was a larger success than he realized. During the next year Jedediah Smith
traveled from the Great Salt Lake to California and back. Lean, weather-stained men
in buckskin were riding through every nook
and corner of the Rocky Mountain country.
The trails by which a restless people were to
take their wagon outfits westward were being
beaten down; the same trails by which to-day
we travel in railway train and automobile.

STEPHEN FULLER AUSTIN

THIS is the story of Stephen F. Austin, an idealist, who took hold of a real-estate proposition and built from it a nation. Brief of stature and slight of form—a wiry man those who knew him described him—with the large deep eyes and the high forehead of one who sees beyond to-day's horizon. And gently reared, although it was on the frontier. For his father, Moses Austin, owned a smelter in the little village of Potosi, fifty miles or so south of St. Louis, and the business did so well in the days before the War of 1812 that the son was sent East, first to private school and then to college. With visions of a career as an orator, he returned to the raw young State of Missouri and served two terms in its legislature. Then the paper-money smash came; banks failed everywhere; the lead mines closed; the smelter shut down; the village of Potosi went to sleep. Moses Austin lost his fortune, and Stephen went down the Mississippi looking for a job.

Twenty-seven years old, willing to try anything once, as we say now; he served a term
as circuit judge, riding from court to court
in the backwoods of Arkansas; he drifted on,
seeking work as a clerk at steamboat-landings,
visiting one plantation after another to offer
his services as an overseer. In New Orleans
he finally ran across Joseph H. Hawkins,
brother of a former schoolmate, who started
to teach him more law and gave him his
board. Here he was enlarging his prospects a
little by doing some poorly paid newspaper
work on the side, when he found himself heir
to his father's heavy debts and the large idea
of Texas.

It came about in this way: Moses Austin
was a pioneer and, long before the hard times
descended, he had been itching for a new try
at the wilderness. Those were the days of the
great land hunger, when it seemed as if half
the people in this country were traveling by
flatboats down the long Ohio and by covered Conestoga wagons down the deeply
rutted roads that led into the West. Free
land: that was the lure. And the Government
at Washington was putting up the price—a
dollar and a quarter an acre, cash down, now.

The speculators were getting hold of the best tracts. But out beyond the Sabine River lay the unpeopled holdings of Spain. You saw them through a golden mist of legends— legends of riches and power to be gained by wild adventure. Down in New Orleans, bold-eyed gentlemen with wide-rimmed hats and long cigars were organizing expeditions to make their fortunes by smuggling in slaves across that *terra incognita* from the Gulf coast and by founding empires on its prairies. Jean Lafitte, like a king, was still ruling his pirate settlement on Galveston Island. The neutral strip just beyond the Sabine was a sanctuary for runaway negroes, river pirates and mur-derers. The road from Natchidoches, Louisi-ana's western outpost, reached four hundred miles to San Antonio—and hardly a white man along it. Now and again a trader came back by this lonely trail with tales of the sleeping Spanish village and the rich lands intervening.

Rich lands and people hungry for free acres. Moses Austin had been restless in the prosperous years at Potosi. In these days of his bankruptcy he saw his opportunity. And in the fifty-third year of his life he set forth, undaunted, to seize it. A long and weary journey, and when he came to the little town of flat-roofed adobes near the ruined stone mission which men called the Alamo, the Spanish governor Martinez told him to turn around and go back home at once, unless he wanted to land in jail. But it happened that the Baron de Bastrop, one time of Prussia, now a citizen of Spain, met him at the governor's doorway and befriended him, with the result that when he started home he had his grant. Free lands on which to settle three hundred families; the right to rule his colony and to take a cash fee of twelve and a half cents an acre from every member. In the rough, what his share would amount to was eighteen thousand dollars and a large tract of his own. But while he was making the homeward journey with this good news, Moses Austin was deserted by the trader who was his companion; on top of this his powder got wet. So, for weeks, he lived on acorns. What with the exposure and his years, it was too much for him. He returned to the home of a married daughter near Little Rock, Arkansas, sick unto death. During those last days he sent word to his son Stephen of what he had done, bidding him carry on.

Now eighteen thousand dollars was a great deal of money in that year of 1821. And eighteen thousand dollars was the foremost idea in Stephen Austin's mind when he set forth from New Orleans for the drowsy town of Natchidoches with its convent where the mocking-birds sang in the blossom-laden trees at the edge of No Man's Land. To pay his father's debts and to rehabilitate the family fortunes—that was the way the proposition looked then.

A little money, borrowed from his benefactor, Joseph Hawkins, in his belt; a little company of traders for his companions when he left Natchidoches for the neutral strip, where wanted men were thick and a few settlers were reaping their first crop of corn. On the first day out he got word of his father's death, and in that same package of mail there came confirmation of Governor Martinez's grant.

Horseback across hundreds of miles of prairies and wooded river bottoms. It was July and game was plentiful. But in itself the wilderness held no lure for him. He looked upon the vastness of the prairies and he had a vision of those boundless acres broken by the plows of settlers to grain-yielding fields. That vision helped to harden his slight body to discomforts and to steady his jumping nerves when the fierce discordance of the war-whoop split the night's silence more than once that summer.

In San Antonio he found a people so far removed from their capital that last year's news of laws and politics was barely come this year. He saw a company of ragged Spanish soldiers who used to catch up the ponies of visiting Comanches for the warriors, lest those warriors find displeasure and punish the community by massacre. Governor Martinez was in a receptive mood—a colony of Americans with their long-barreled rifles might help to hold this land, whose settlements had been depopulated, its missions left to ruin and its ranchos laid waste by warlike savages. Austin drew up plans for the government of the future colonists. Then he spent weary weeks, whose monotony of toil and hardship was varied by an occasional brush with the blood-thirsty Caranchua Indians, surveying his

lands with a few companions. The tract lay
between the Colorado (this is the Colorado
which empties into the Gulf of Mexico) and
the Brazos rivers—in the middle of what is
now southern Texas. Autumn had come when
he returned to New Orleans, with his clothes
torn to tatters and his skin stained by wind
and weather. That idea of eighteen thousand
dollars was still abiding in his mind; but with
it there was the vision of a wilderness turned
into farm-lands, of towns where solitudes had
been.

The papers of New Orleans published the
news of what he had done; the papers of other
cities copied it. A flood of letters poured in
from restless farmers, for the most part from
the South. Land-hungry men began to appear.
Austin spent several busy weeks answering
inquiries and buying supplies. He borrowed
more money from Joseph Hawkins; outfitted
a little schooner which sailed away from New
Orleans for the mouth of the Colorado River
with a score of passengers, and he himself set
out overland with Josiah Bell, a surveyor,
and a number of farmers. The settlement of
Texas was begun.

In the autumn of 1821 he arrived at San

Antonio. He put in weary months with Josiah Bell locating his handful of settlers in the cane-brake bottoms of the Colorado. And other months—wearier and more discouraging—searching for the party whom the schooner was to have landed at the river's mouth. For the little vessel's captain had missed his bearings and, while Austin was looking for them, the passengers were wandering along the lower Brazos, which had been mistaken for the Colorado. Then, in the midst of this game of hide and seek, Austin got word that the officials down in Mexico did not approve of the plan which he and Governor Martinez had worked out. If he wanted his grant he had to begin all over again.

He left his surveyor, Josiah Bell, to look after the sadly scattered colonists in this wilderness and with a little less than four hundred dollars in his pocket he started overland for the City of Mexico. Before he reached the Rio Grande a band of Comanches captured him, but he talked them into releasing him. By disguising himself as a common laborer he escaped the bandits who were robbing and murdering along the road. And when he reached the capital he found that Mexico had seceded from Spain.

A nation in the throes of its beginnings; rival factions; revolutions and counter-revolutions. All this turmoil about him and he knew only some twenty words of Spanish. He spent a year down there. His money went. He pawned his watch; he sold part of his scanty wardrobe; he borrowed from new acquaintances among the Europeans in the city. Some days he did not eat. He found it hard to pay the postage on such letters as he had to write. Meantime, he learned the language. He induced a congress which was sweating and fighting over a national constitution to attend to the details of this land grant of his —in a wilderness so far away that many members of the congress had never heard of it. By the new terms the fees which he was to get from the colonists would barely cover the costs of surveying and location. In other words, that eighteen thousand dollars which was to have paid his father's debts and set him on his feet was gone a-glimmering. All he had coming to him for his work was a large tract of land. But the project was assured. Forty-five hundred acres for a family;

fifteen hundred acres to a single man; self-government in local affairs; himself at the head. With these provisions, secured by un-remitting toil and skilled diplomacy, he felt that Texas was established. And Texas had become his dream. What did the eighteen thousand dollars matter? He could wait for that.

So he returned to his wilderness. Most of the families who had come by the unlucky schooner had departed eastward after months of starvation and hardship. The mail which awaited him at San Antonio told of rumors throughout the States of his project's failure. By the next post to New Orleans he sent a broadside of what real-estate promoters now call literature. He settled down to work, es-tablishing a government, planting a town called San Felipe de Austin on the lower Brazos, adjusting differences among his half-hundred families along the river bottom, re-cording tracts, making himself stronger with the governor at San Antonio. The months went by. New letters of inquiry came in. And then new settlers. Some came by schooner; many more by covered wagons crawling along the road from Natchidoches.

Oftentimes, when his surveyor was busy, Austin himself ran the lines for their holdings. Many of them had no money to pay for the surveying and recording. If they had it, he took a little down; the balance later. Corn, cows, wild honey, smoke-tanned buckskin or beeswax; these were usually his fees. He lived in a log cabin when he was home—dirt floor and, for a long while, no windows. Corn bread, coffee made of parched corn, game for meat. He did his own cooking—when he had time. By the light of blazing pine splinters he wrote out the records of new tracts, he kept his books, and turned out long letters to the papers of a dozen States back East. Many a midnight found him bent over the table of split boards, with the pen in his cramped fingers.

Now the caliber of the men and women who were to take these free lands was the main ingredient in Stephen Austin's problem at this time. He wanted only those who were going to stick it out. By the terms of his grant the colonists must become citizens of Mexico. They must comply with the established church, which was the Catholic. And slavery was prohibited by the Constitution. The average land-seeker of those days was enthusiastic in his Americanism, to put it mildly. The great majority were Protestants. Many of them were slave-owners, to whom this venture would be impossible unless they could bring their negroes.

On the one side the Mexican laws and officials—on the other these people of a stubborn breed and dissenting ideas. Austin set to work to secure harmony between the two. The restrictions, which many a man would conveniently have forgotten to mention in his advertising, he rather emphasized in his long letters to eastern papers and to applicants. Those who came, came with full understanding. And, at the same time, by astute and tireless maneuvering which would have done credit to an Old World diplomat, he managed to wring from the Mexican authorities a large tolerance in the enforcement of the state religion; he got a modification of the law so that the southerners could bring in their negroes. It was his right to pass on every applicant. He took good care to exclude all who came with hopes of speculation. Of filibusters and annexationists, none stood a chance with him.

Men and women who would stick it out. That idea was always uppermost. The wilderness was no joke. He insisted on references as to responsibility and moral fiber. He passed on these rigidly. And he got the men and women whom he wanted. How some of them managed to stick it out during those first years is a mystery; but they did it.

There are men living to-day down in Texas who have heard old-timers tell the story of those early days, and the tale, as they repeat it, is a brave one. Grass-covered prairies stretching on to the horizon. Wide river bottoms, with thick forest and dense cane-brakes. That was the land. They started in along the river bottoms. Hard-working men who wore their powder-horns almost as constantly as you and I wear our watch-chains, who carried their long-barreled rifles across their plow-handles and placed them beside their home-made stools at meal-times. Patient women with hands that grew calloused at the ax and hoe, with eyes that grew quick searching the thickets beyond the doorstep where the children played, for signs of Indians; with breasts that grew lean under the ache that comes when there is no milk for yearning

little lips. They burned away patches in the
cane-brakes and they cleared away patches in
the forests. Many had no plows; they drilled
holes in the stubborn earth with sharpened
sticks and planted corn. They built log cabins;
dirt floors and no windows; pole-and-clay
roofs which let in the rain. Nine months without the sight of bread—that was a common
story. When the first scanty crops came, the
women pounded the corn to meal in stone
mortars. They dug roots and ground acorns.
Game, for the most part, was their food. Often the game was scarce. Many a family
learned to relish the meat of the wild mus-
tangs. In most places they kept their cabins
close together for fear of the Indians. It was
the custom of some of the men to stay on
guard while others hunted. And when the
hunters returned in the evening the children
always came out to meet them, solemn-eyed
and silent, looking to see whether there was
food that night. Coffee and tea and sugar
were unknown. Years after Texas was a nation there were families using parched corn
as a substitute for coffee. New babies came.
They came in windowless cabins with earthen
floors. And the mother who had the help of

another woman in her great hour was more fortunate than most of her sisters.

Always the Indians. To the north and west the Comanches, fierce lords of the Llano Estacado and the wide prairies; to the east the Wacos and the Kickapoos; to the south the bloody Caranchuas. More than fifty years of massacre and midnight raid; that is one chapter in the story of Texas, and the chapter opened with tragedy enough to fill a book.

Life in these cabins among the cane-brakes and the forests along the Colorado and the Brazos bottoms was just about as uncertain a proposition as life in the caves of prehistoric man. Take the family of Claiborne Wright during their first year on lower Red River. There was not powder enough in their log hut to last through one of the all-night fights which almost every one had to expect sooner or later. So they built a raft of driftwood. Every evening, when darkness came, the mother and the two little girls got on this raft; the father and the three boys swam behind it, pushing it across the stream. And they hid there in the cane thickets until morning.

Joseph Taylor and his family were lucky

enough to have plenty of powder on the November night when a band of Kickapoos attacked their cabin on Little River. All the time the fight was going on the two girls were molding bullets on the hearthstone. The youngest boy—a twelve-year-old—shot down two Indians. When the savages set fire to the house the mother crawled out on the roof and stayed there, with arrows rattling all around her, until she put out the flames. Meanwhile the father and the two boys took such heavy toll with their long-barreled rifles through the loopholed windows that the naked warriors retired.

You can find a hundred other stories like these if you choose to comb through annals of those early years. And as the farm-lands spread, as one tribe and another were subdued by fierce reprisals, throughout the years there still continued to be a frontier with new hostile tribes beyond. During all their other struggles for existence these people were forever busy fighting Indians.

In a biography of Sam Houston there is a quotation from Ralph Waldo Emerson describing the American frontiersman which will stand repetition here. "So tenacious a stock that, if it were transplanted on a slab of marble, it would take root and grow."

These early families took root. And, as they grew, more families came. In two years Stephen Austin was able to secure for them from Mexico a form of self-government to replace his own benevolent dictatorship. At the end of another year his contract was fulfilled; he had three hundred families; and he got another contract for an adjoining tract. Incidentally, he was poorer in this world's goods than when he had begun. For the future, he saw little hope of wealth. But if Texas was to continue growing, some one had to look after it. And Texas had become the dearest thing in life to him.

So he kept on. Days in the saddle lining out new settlers to their lands. Long expeditions against the hostile Indians. Weary journeys down across the Rio Grande to Saltillo, the capital of Coahuila, to which province Texas belonged. Never a week passed without bringing some dispute for him to settle. Quarrels over land boundaries, family rows, clashes between communities and the authorities, and the inevitable collisions between

American frontiersmen and a government founded on Latin customs. He attended to them all. He advised farmers as to what crops to plant; he picked names for new babies; sentenced horse-thieves to the whipping-post; wrote laws into the statute-books of Mexico; and played the game of international politics between times.

For Texas was growing fast and surely now. Five hundred families in 1825; in 1827 one hundred more, and in 1828 another three hundred. In all, twelve hundred homes established through his efforts. Towns were springing up. They had a school at San Felipe de Austin. With this growth in the area which he had gotten between the Brazos and the Colorado, there had come wider interest east of the Mississippi. Back there the desire was increasing to annex Texas to the United States. President Andrew Jackson had already offered Mexico a million dollars for it. And this desire was bringing a new type of settlers. Men who had no idea of becoming citizens of Mexico, whose hope was for secession; they came to other colonies which had begun to grow up alongside Austin's. Near the town of Nacogdoches, in the neutral strip, some of them tried to stage a little revolution. Now Mexico had seen a deal of revolution lately and, naturally enough, she began to fear that this abortive effort was not going to be the last.

So in the year 1830 things began to happen. The Mexican congress passed a decree forbidding further immigration from America; it sent troops of ex-convict soldiers to the settlements north of the Rio Grande and put the people virtually under martial law. Austin saw the ruin and end of his colony if this were not stopped. He put in the next few months bringing to bear all the pressure he could upon high officials and got what amounted to a nullification of the statutes so far as his colony was concerned. But in the meantime the soldiers had come; clashes had occurred down on the Gulf coast between these troops and the citizens. The fire was kindled, and the man did not live who could stamp it out.

Texas was part of the state of Coahuila. Now the settlers wanted separation. In San Felipe de Austin they held a convention and drew up a proposed constitution; they named three delegates to go down to the City of Mexico and present their petition. Of these

three Stephen Austin was one; he was the
only one who went. A revolution and an epidemic of black cholera were going on at the
same time in the capital. Somehow he managed to escape the bullets and the sickness;
but in the end he lost his temper, and during
an interview with the vice-president he said
that Texas was surely going to get self-government sooner or later. These words landed
him in jail.

High treason was the charge. A cell in the
old prison of the inquisition was his quarters.
And *incomunicado* was the rule applied to
him, which meant that he saw no one and was
allowed to send out no word. So for three
months: stone walls, stone floor and, for only
two hours a day, enough light for him to see
his grim surroundings. This blessed surcease
of time he employed in drawing pictures of
Texas landscape on the wall with a bit of
charcoal from the fireplace. After the three
months they took him to a better prison and
allowed him visitors. But he could get no
trial. For two years he remained in custody;
and then Santa Anna, who had ridden on the
wave of the last revolution into his dictatorship, set him free.

To put it very briefly, those two things were the causes of the Texan revolution—the imprisonment of Stephen Austin and the refusal of Mexico to grant separate statehood. But the underlying reason, by which the conflict was inevitable, was the fundamental difference between these settlers and the people south of the Rio Grande. And when Austin returned to Texas after his two years in jail the fight was as good as on.

Out of the turmoil of attempted martial law, of incompetent officials—some of whom, by the way, were Americans sent out from the City of Mexico—and of rigid restrictive statutes, there had arisen a new set of leaders in the colony. William B. Travis, a young South Carolina lawyer; Sam Houston, one time governor of Tennessee, who had come West to live among the Indians; James Bowie, William Wharton, Branch Archer and a half-dozen others—typical Americans, intolerant lovers of self-government. Separation from Coahuila or secession—that was their cry. Down in the City of Mexico Santa Anna, the new dictator, was sending new troops northward to make these troublesome Americans keep quiet. In days gone by Austin had hung

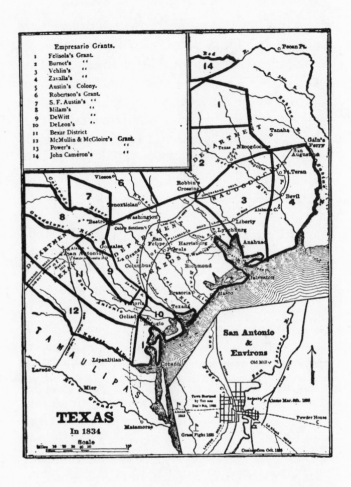

Empresario Grants.

1. Felisola's Grant.
2. Burnet's "
3. Vehlin's "
4. Zavalla's "
5. Austin's Colony.
6. Robertson's Grant.
7. S. F. Austin's "
8. Milam's "
9. DeWitt "
10. DeLeon's "
11. Bexar District
12. McMullin & McGloire's Grant.
13. Power's "
14. John Cameron's "

TEXAS

In 1834

Scale

to the determination that this colony should remain a part of Mexico. Now the day came when he saw that if Texas were going to live she must secede. Forthwith he joined forces with these men whom he had bitterly opposed before and became a revolutionist.

It was late in the year 1835 when the fighting started. Just west of Austin's grants a Missourian of the name of Green De Witt had established a colony in which there was a little town of thirty cabins, called Gonzales. This hamlet had managed to survive several years of fierce warfare with the Indians. The citizens had borrowed a miserable little brass cannon from the Mexican officials to help stand off the savages. With the arrival of the first troops from south of the Rio Grande the Mexicans demanded the return of the field-piece. The people of Gonzales refused; two companies of soldiers advanced upon the town. And a handful of ragged Texans sent them back to San Antonio on the run. When Santa Anna got the news, he prepared to clear Texas of Americans.

For the warfare which followed there is no space in this brief tale beyond the barest outline. Early in the game the Texans took the town of San Antonio against odds of ten to one. Under the command of Santa Anna more than three thousand Mexican troops found William Barret Travis holding the place with one hundred and eighty-two untrained men. These had taken refuge in the walled yard of the Alamo chapel. One Sunday morning in the month of March the Mexicans stormed those adobe walls, and the Texans, who could have stolen away at any time during the siege had they so chosen, died to the last man. For every one of those still forms there were more than three dead Mexicans lying in the blood and muck of that three-acre space when the dour smoke clouds cleared away that Sunday morning. Shortly afterward Santa Anna surrounded four hundred Texans under Colonel J. W. Fannin down at Goliad near the Gulf coast, and, after their surrender, shot them down. Then, when all the families in western and central Texas were fleeing for the Sabine River, Sam Houston whipped the ragged little army into shape. After a long retreat, all the way from San Antonio to Galveston Bay, this raw-boned strategist of the frontier turned suddenly at the mouth of the San Jacinto River.

In less than a half-hour eight hundred of Stephen Austin's transplanted farmers had defeated thirteen hundred regulars. The Mexicans surrendered; Santa Anna was captured, trying to escape. The revolution was over.

In the battles Stephen Austin took no part. Early in the game the Texas revolutionary council realized that it took money to carry on a war. So they sent him east with William H. Wharton and Branch Archer to raise funds. New Orleans first; then up the Mississippi to St. Louis, and at every little river town where the steamer stopped they spread the propaganda of Texas freedom. From St. Louis eastward. On to Washington. Behind them they left enthusiasm. Companies of volunteers enlisted and sailed for Texas. Where they went the envoys borrowed right and left. Word came slowly in those days; of what was going on at home they had no idea. The Alamo was already a glorious memory by the time they heard of it; the massacre of Fannin's men at Goliad reached them as fresh news when Sam Houston was defeating Santa Anna's armies at San Jacinto. So, always, they worked in the darkness of fearful doubt;

but they kept on working—and they raised the money which made it possible for Texas to become a nation. More than that—they raised the storm of sympathy by whose endurance in the years to come their little nation gained its recognition from the various world powers.

When he came home Stephen Austin found a new leader risen to the place which he had held among these people whom he had brought to the wilderness. At the first presidential election he was persuaded to be a candidate. General Sam Houston, with the glamour of San Jacinto about his big raw-boned form, snowed him under by an overwhelming vote. For the first time since he had left New Orleans to carry out his father's real-estate proposition, Austin thought of taking a rest. To retire to some of his lands and go to stock-raising; that was his idea. It was short-lived. For Houston asked him to serve as secretary of state.

If Texas were to live as a nation she must get recognition. To get that recognition from the older, greater nations, she needed one who was a diplomat. And Stephen Austin not only was a diplomat but one who knew well the ins and outs of those questions which must be

Sam Houston

debated by long correspondence with foreign cabinets. So, reluctantly, he took up the work.

The capital of Texas was for the time at the raw hamlet of Columbia down on the Brazos. A handful of log cabins and split clapboard houses. In one of these he had his quarters. And he was a sick man, worn out by years of work and hardship. It was in the winter and a norther blew down across the prairies. A cold which had settled upon his lungs developed into pneumonia. When he could work no longer, he took to his bed.

A pallet bed upon a puncheon floor. A drafty room. Always in his mind the work which was to be done for Texas. One night he rose and tried to do some writing. Then he crept back into his blankets and delirium came upon him. Two or three friends were giving him what help they could. One of them was sitting by his bedside when Stephen Austin awakened from his fevered dreams. He awakened, but so strong was the vision which had come to him that it persisted now. And his voice, for all its weakness, had a ring of joy.

"Texas is recognized," he said. "The news just came."

Then with that dream upon him he sank back and died. Forty-three years of age. His lands barely paid his debts. He had started with an idea of making money. The idea had grown into an ideal; and the ideal had mastered him. One after another he had seen his visions come true. And the last of them, with which death found him, was realized in a few years. Texas was recognized. A little nation, short of life and pitifully poor, she came at last to us, bringing, together with the great Southwest and California, the proud tradition of the Alamo, born in the reek and din and blood of battle, standing perhaps unequaled in the world's brave annals.

THE ALAMO HAD NONE

FOR more than two thousand years the stand of Leonidas and his Spartans had been unrivaled in the proud annals of arms. Then the men of the Alamo went to their deaths and the world had a new tradition, finer even than the old tale of Thermopylæ.

The heroes of other mighty chapters in history held their ground in disciplined obedience. These warriors of the new-born nation of Texas knew no discipline; they submitted to no man's command. They came to their great hour by their own wills. When they had their choice of surrender, retreat or death, they raised their hands and swore that they would neither yield nor flee. Through twelve days and nights and the last bloody dawn, when thousands swarmed upon them, every man of them kept that oath.

Most of them were settlers who had left their wives and children to hold their lonely cabins against hostile Indians; a ragged lot, sunburned, lank-haired, unshaven; the shoes of many gaped at the toes and some were shod in moccasins. There were a goodly number of professional filibusters: soldiers of fortune who had drifted along the Gulf coast from New Orleans, to try their luck in half a dozen revolutions; a hard-eyed crowd who knew the smell of powder smoke and, oftentimes, the smell of Mexican jails. There was a sprinkling of young professional men from Louisiana and other Southern States: restless souls to whom the orations of Patrick Henry were as divine revelations. But few of these soldiers abided in the Alamo, for the streets of San Antonio offered them some relaxation; and there was a chance to get a bite to eat— or a bit to drink—among the flat-topped adobe houses.

They had captured this walled inclosure across the river from San Antonio in the fall. They were holding it and the town against the Mexicans—the western outpost of the young nation of Texas in her war of independence. Colonel J. C. Neill was their commanding officer.

It was early in January, 1836, when William Barret Travis came to take command of them. Twenty-eight years of age; tall and handsome; every inch a gentleman; one of those soft-voiced southerners in whom the love of liberty was a living passion.

Now there was one thing on which the majority of the garrison were united. It was their high regard for Lieutenant-Colonel James Bowie, who had taken a man's part in the capture of this place a few weeks before and was still here. So, when they heard that Travis had arrived, more than one hundred of them took their rifles and marched from town to the Alamo. They called Neill from his quarters and told him that, unless he turned over the command to Bowie, they were going to lynch him. The sick man did the best he could under the circumstances, which was to issue an order giving joint authority to Bowie and Travis.

Then Neill departed and the two rivals met to discuss the uninspiring situation. Southerners both, for the one a deadly knife was named; the other had nearly worn his Bible out—Bowie the burly man of middle age, duelist, filibuster and Indian-fighter; something of a scholar, polished as the best of them in a drawing-room and rough and ready as the worst of them in the powder smoke:

Travis, auburn-haired and barely twenty-eight, always a student, soft of voice and somewhat diffident, until he faced a crowd or action came. Just what they said has not come down, but when they got through it was with the agreement to sign all orders jointly. And that same day they fixed their signatures to a letter telling the governor and council that Santa Anna's army was drawing near; asking for reinforcements to be sent at once.

But the governor and the council were fighting bitterly over the question of authority, and General Sam Houston, who was in command of the pitiful little Texan army, had been recalled from the field. Most of the few troops were off on a wild-goose-chase under Colonel J. W. Fannin down near Matagorda Bay. So the days went by and the weeks wore into months; no reinforcements came.

By the middle of February definite tidings of Santa Anna's army began to reach them: three or four thousand soldiers near the Rio Grande, with the dictator at their head. It was now evident that the handful of Texans in San Antonio were going to get no help before these thousands swarmed upon them. Travis and Bowie—who had no more reasons to like each other than the governor and the council back in San Felipe—talked the matter over. The road to the east stretched away across the river bottom; you could see it from the Alamo where it climbed the low bluffs, and it must have looked inviting to these two southern gentlemen. For all their antagonism they were in complete agreement as to the invitation which it extended. If the garrison could hang on long enough, there was a chance that those whom they were defending might yet understand the grim emergency and send more men to them. If that chance failed—they would, at least, have done the best they could. So they agreed to stick it out.

They picked the Alamo as the spot to make their stand. The stone church and the walled convent yard near-by offered good cover. There were fourteen cannon here, left by the Mexicans at the taking of San Antonio some weeks before. Two old artillery sergeants, who had served with the regular army, set a number of men to work rearranging the ordnance. A party was detailed to dig a well inside the yard. There was a large breach in the north wall which should be mended, and provisions were needed to withstand a siege.

But no officer could order a private to labor and get obedience unless the private chose. So the breach remained unmended and no food was gathered; the well was only half-completed and the arrangement of the cannon was barely finished before the final alarm came.

The day—it was the twenty-second of February—had passed in San Antonio very much like the other days preceding it. Most of the men were in town, and more than one of them was deep in drink this afternoon when the bells of the churches clanged the alarm. Santa Anna's army was approaching from the west on the old Laredo road. As the Texans hurried through the streets between the flat-roofed adobe houses a scattering of townspeople followed them across the little river.

The enemy were in the western outskirts before they got across the bridge, and as the last fugitives entered the gateway at the south end of the convent yard the air was shaking with the dull thunder of Santa Anna's cannon.

Here in the three-acre inclosure where the brown-robed Franciscan fathers used to teach Indian neophytes to read and write, to weave and sew in days long gone, sunburned settlers, tobacco-chewing southerners and bold-eyed

THE ALAMO, SAN ANTONIO, TEXAS

filibusters from two hemispheres were jostling one another. The thick stone walls which had once echoed the thin sweet treble of childish voices, intoned to old Latin hymns, gave back a roaring cacophony in deep bass, topped now and then by a fierce high note as some rowdy who was searching for his missing rifle cursed his carelessness.

There was a stone building with a veranda running the length of its second floor on the eastern side of the yard. Most of the officers were gathered on the porch in council, for some one had seen a white flag on the river bridge. Bowie advocated sending a party in answer to this truce signal, but Travis bitterly opposed it. The discussion did not last long, for Bowie soon took the law into his own hands. He hurried to the bridge with a few men, bearing a white handkerchief on a staff. In less than a half-hour he returned. Santa Anna had demanded the immediate surrender of the garrison; otherwise no quarter would be given any one inside the walls.

Then Travis stepped to the edge of the veranda. He raised his hand for silence. The tumult in the long yard died away. He began to speak.

His words have not come down. All that remains for memory of that oration is the picture: the tall young speaker, with his auburn hair, his gray eyes ablaze; the lake of upturned faces, every one of them intent. More than one member of that audience had bidden profane defiance to the officers; many a man down there was still unsteady on his feet from drink; and there were some who had traded off their rifles for whisky that same week in San Antonio. Only a short time ago the most of them had threatened to lynch their colonel if he turned over the command to this man who was now speaking. But when Travis came to the end of his oration a thing took place which will be remembered as long as there is any glory in the tradition of arms and men.

As yet, he said, the way was open for those who chose to go. But he had a demand to make from those who stayed. He bade these to raise their hands and swear to stick it out to the very last. There were one hundred and fifty-six men in the garrison. One hundred and fifty-six men raised their hands to take that oath.

Then most of the townspeople went back

to San Antonio. There remained, of the non-combatants, Mrs. Almiram Dickinson, whose husband, a lieutenant in the garrison, had taken her and her baby behind him on his horse across the river when the enemy were entering the town; the Mexican wife of Dr. Allsbury, who was down near Matagorda Bay with Fannin's troops; her sister and a negro slave. The atrocities which Santa Anna had committed in recent revolutions down across the Rio Grande were sufficient reason for any woman with relatives among the rebels to keep out of San Antonio just now.

Evening was coming down. Bowie took twenty-five men and began a search of the scattering houses along this side of the river for provisions; a detachment went to work finishing the half-completed well; Captain Juan Seguin, one of the few Mexicans who were loyal to the Texan cause, and eight vaqueros were driving a score of cattle into a picket corral beside the east wall. A tremendous change had come over the place. In all the hurried movement there was now none of that disorder which had been predominant before. Discord had gone. The very drunkards were sober, coolly waiting orders at their posts.

That night the tramp of horses and the dull rattle of wheels were heard. The dawn came and, with the growing light, the thunder of artillery. Shells began to drop into the convent yard. Under the drifting smoke-wreaths at the edge of the town, five hundred yards away, the sentries could see the Mexican soldiers serving two batteries. A score of men found vantage points along the wall; their rifles made a thin, dry answer to the salvos, an eighteen-pounder bellowed from the yard. The din along the river bank diminished. The Mexican field-pieces were whirled away to safety.

The darkness of the next night seemed to be alive with sounds; they came from all four sides: remote stirrings, mysterious as the breeze which carried them; the clank of caisson wheels; the thudding undernote of horsemen moving through the gloom. On the morning of the twenty-fourth the men of Texas found themselves surrounded by infantry, artillery and cavalry. Above the belfry of the largest church in San Antonio, less than a mile away, they saw . blood-red flag. It meant No Quarter.

That night one of Captain Juan Seguin's

vaqueros slipped through the Mexican lines
on a fast horse and struck out for San Felipe
with a letter.

"To the people of Texas and all Americans
in the world," so the message was addressed.
And it went on:

Fellow citizens and compatriots—I am be-
sieged by a thousand or more of the Mexicans
under Santa Anna—I have sustained a continual
Bombardment and cannonade for 24 hours and
have not lost a man— The enemy has demanded
a surrender at discretion, otherwise, the garrison
are to be put to the sword, if the fort is taken—I
have answered the demand with a cannon shot,
and our flag still waves proudly from the walls
—*I shall never surrender or retreat. Then,* I call
on you in the name of Liberty, of patriotism and
everything dear to the American character, to
come to our aid with all dispatch— The enemy
is receiving reinforcements daily and will no doubt
increase to three or four thousand in four or five
days. If this call is neglected, I am determined to
sustain myself as long as possible and die like a
soldier who never forgets what is due to his own
honor and that of his country— VICTORY OR
DEATH.

WILLIAM BARRET TRAVIS
P. S. The Lord is on our side— When the

enemy appeared in sight we had not three bushels of corn— We have since found in deserted houses 80 or 90 bushels and got into the walls 20 or 30 head of Beeves.   TRAVIS

The vaquero who took that letter left the Alamo by the road leading to the east. An outpost of Santa Anna's cavalry were the only troops then guarding this wagon track. In the garrison were more than twenty men familiar with every foot of the ground here. They could have guided their companions out to safety—any night. They could have slipped away themselves. But the only ones who sought that road were the messengers sent out from time to time with pleas for reinforcements.

On the second day of the siege, when pneumonia had a tight grip on him and he should have been in bed, James Bowie was commanding a squad who were setting a cannon on an emplacement. Standing on a scaffolding, he missed his footing and fell. They carried him to his cot in a one-story stone building beside the south gate of the yard. His hip was broken. Fever came and then delirium. The three women who had their quarters in the partly ruined church close by, because of its isolation from the fighting in case of assault, took turns in coming in to nurse him and the other sick.

By the third day two of Santa Anna's batteries were sheltered behind earthworks on the other side of the river. From then on they kept up a slow bombardment. Hardly an hour of daylight but a cannon ball fell somewhere within the yard. The men were constantly at work with picks and shovels, reinforcing the walls, mending fresh breaches, building breastworks in the doorways of the stone buildings behind which to make their stand when the final assault should come. Almost every night a party stole out on a sortie against the Mexican lines. And during all of it, by some strange fortune, not one of them was killed. It was as if the fate that had brought them here was saving them to share the one great hour.

The lines of earthworks grew around them. With the coming of every dawn the sentries discovered new intrenchments, until the Alamo was in the center of a nearly unbroken circle, whose circumference was held by infantry, artillery and cavalry. Now and again the sound of marching troops came from the west, to announce the arrival of new regiments. The number of the enemy had grown to between three and four thousand men.

Time dragged heavily in the long nights. To while away the hours one of the soldiers used to take his fiddle from its case and play for his companions. That musician was David Crockett, veteran of the War of 1812, famous as a frontiersman and Indian-fighter, ex-congressman from Tennessee. In his fifty-first year he had turned his back on ease and renown to come out here and fight for freedom as a private in the Texan army. Perhaps you can picture him—lean and gray-haired, in his buckskin hunting-shirt and fringed leggings, sawing away to some old jig tune, with the ring of sunburned faces about him and the sentry glancing down upon them from the walls.

Always, during these days, some one was looking up that road which led over the low bluffs to the east, searching the sky-line for the dust of advancing reinforcements. Always the sky-line remained unchanged. And always to the west the blood-red banner flapped lazily from the cupola of the church across the river.

David Crockett

One night when it seemed evident that the governor and council at San Felipe were not going to send any help, Travis called James Butler Bonham to his quarters. The two had grown up together as boys in North Carolina; as young men they had practised law together in an Alabama village. And after Travis had come to Texas, seeking to better his fortunes, Bonham had followed him. They had a talk together; and that night Bonham rode away from the Alamo on a fast horse, to seek for reinforcements.

Several days went by. No word had come from Bonham. It began to look as if he might have been captured by the Mexicans. On the night of February 29 Travis called a council of officers. They picked Juan Seguin because of his nationality as the best man to elude Santa Anna's sentries and to carry out another plea for help. The fastest horse within the walls belonged to James Bowie. When Seguin went to ask for the animal, the sick man was barely able to recognize him. Departing by a breach in the north wall, the Spaniard was challenged by a sentry who expressed a profanely small opinion of any one who would leave his comrades at such a time. The man changed his growling into a "Good luck to you!" when the nature of the errand was explained. A troop of Santa Anna's cavalry guarded the eastward road. Seguin had a vaquero with him. The two of them approached the sentries at a walk, answered their challenge in Spanish; and, when they were almost within arm's length, clapped spurs to their horses. They burst through the lines and raced on up the road with the bullets snarling around them. Their objective was Fannin's troops down near the Gulf; but when they were two days out they met an officer who told them that James Butler Bonham had preceded them; that Fannin had held a council of war, which had ruled against sending reinforcements. So Seguin went on to San Felipe to plead with the governor and council. Of the original garrison he and his vaquero were the last to leave the Alamo's walls.

But reinforcements came. And, in all the annals of arms and men, there is no story finer than this incident.

On his way to Fannin's camp, young Bonham had passed through Gonzales. It was a pitiful little village; thirty cabins built of split oak boards; the most of them had only one room; their floors were beaten earth. There was a public square in the middle of the place, and when the messenger arrived the people turned out there to hear his tidings. He stopped long enough to tell them of the hard case of the garrison before he rode on.

Then the men of Gonzales organized a company. There were thirty homes in the place. There were thirty-two men in that company. The most of them were still in their twenties and their early thirties—married men, with children in those split-plank cabins. There were a few gray-haired old-timers and one or two boys with the down still soft on their cheeks. They elected Albert Martin as their captain and got J. W. Smith to guide them to the Alamo. When they reached the low bluffs overlooking San Antonio, Smith showed them the Mexican troops—infantry, artillery, cavalry; he pointed out the wide circle of intrenchments and in its center the stone chapel with the walled convent yard close by. They could see the blood-red banner waving from the church across the river. It took no military knowledge to understand that that garrison was doomed to the last man. But when darkness came, these ragged men of Gonzales crept like Indians through Santa Anna's lines and entered the Alamo. To die along with their countrymen!

It was the third of March when young James Butler Bonham came back from Fannin's camp to the line of hills where these men of Gonzales had lain awaiting night, forty-eight hours before. He was weary from hard riding. The discouragement of his bad news was all the company he had. What good could he do by going on? he might well ask himself. Perhaps he did. But if he did, he had an answer. For in the hour after midnight he stole by the Mexican sentries and passed within the walls to join his friends.

At three o'clock that same morning Travis sent J. W. Smith, who had guided in the Gonzales company, with his last letter to the governor and council. After that the men of Texas settled down to await the end. During the next two days many callers came to the arched room in the stone church where the women had their quarters. They came with watches, lockets, worn old letters, and with ill-written notes, which they left with Mrs.

Dickinson to send to those back home when they had died.

Eleven days and nights of waiting had passed. In the hour before the red dawn of Sunday, March the sixth, more than three thousand Mexicans closed in for the final assault. One hundred and seventy-odd able-bodied men were waiting for them. Of the others, some were sick and some had been sent out as couriers.

To get a picture of the place, look at the map on the next page.

Black dark; and the deep dull chill which strikes in to the very soul was in the air. The muffled beat of many feet was audible out there in the surrounding night. The sentries gave the alarm; the men of Texas took their places. The sounds continued, now on this side, now on the other; the shuffling, dead reverberation of some battalion wheeling into position; the faint jingle of accouterments; the neighing of a horse. The blackness turned to gray; the grayness was growing thin; the white line of the dawn began to show above the eastern horizon. A bugle blared; one strident note, brief as a yell of hate.

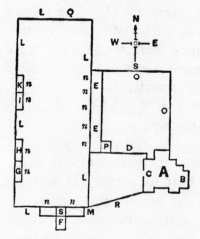

GROUND PLAN OF THE ALAMO.

Now from the north and west and south there came the tramp of approaching thousands. The brazen music of a band rose high above that sullen undernote. It was an air to make one's blood change pace. March music —"El Degüello" was its name; it meant no quarter.

The Texans were scattered along the roofs of the low buildings and the summit of the wall; they were behind the breastworks connecting the yard with the church, and in the church itself. James Bowie was lying in a room in the south building, sick unto death. David Crockett was beside a cannon in the middle of the western barrier. Travis was standing close by another cannon at the northwestern corner, with his friend James Bonham.

Down by the river bridge, where the band was playing five hundred yards away, Santa Anna was peeping around the edge of an adobe barn, to see what he could until it might be safe to come nearer.

The attacking columns closed in. They came at double quick and then on the dead run. The rifles of the Texans spat thin streaks of red into the morning twilight. The cannon shook the earth with their thunder. The mighty hour was in its passing.

Eight hundred rushing upon them from the south; eight hundred from the north; eight hundred from the west. Six hundred cavalry ready to close in behind. The long-barreled rifles of the Texans sent their leaden slugs into the thick-packed masses as fast as men could load and press the triggers. The northern assailants wavered and fell back; those to the south broke and took cover behind a number of adobe buildings. But the western columns swept across the open to the wall; they swarmed over the barrier. Then the battalions to the north re-formed; they trampled down the bodies of their dead and dying comrades as they stormed the northeast corner.

Now Travis fell, with a bullet through his forehead, beside the cannon which he was commanding, and Bonham died near-by.

The Mexicans who had retired in the south came out from behind the adobes and joined the rush over the western wall. The outer defenses were lost. The men of Texas retired to the thick-walled stone buildings.

The three women and the baby and the

negro slave were listening to the uproar from the arched room of the stone chapel, when Lieutenant Dickinson burst in upon them. He took his wife in his arms and told her that the Mexicans were inside the inclosure. Then he kissed her and the baby and hurried away to the fighting. It was the last she ever saw of him.

The long convent yard was packed thick with Mexicans. From the doorways which opened on the veranda of the two-story building a withering rifle fire was pouring down upon them. There was one cannon, in the middle of the western wall, which was still uncaptured. Its defenders had turned it about, and it vomited a bunch of canister into the inclosure. The soldiers of Santa Anna surged en masse upon it; and David Crockett went down here with his clubbed rifle in his hands.

Now the storming of the rooms in the stone buildings began. They were carried one by one. A cannon on the western wall was trained upon a doorway. A shot from this piece; a volley of musketry, and then the final rush was made. The hand-to-hand fighting within these stone-walled cubicles was so fierce that often Mexican brained Mexican.

Outside them the dead lay in bloody heaps.

During this period of the struggle James Bowie ended his days in grim glory. He was a dying man when Santa Anna's soldiers surged into the room where he was lying. But Mexicans who afterward saw his body told with awe how one of the dead hands gripped a pistol, and how the bodies of several of their countrymen were sprawling on the earthen floor.

The sound of firing began to diminish. In the shelter of that adobe barn, five hundred yards away, Santa Anna got the idea it would be safe to come closer and see the slaughter. But the gray twilight had lifted, and the handful of Texans who were still left in the ruined church were able to line their sights upon his escort. When the dictator heard the slugs snarling about his ears he hurried back to cover. Nor did he fare forth again until it was too late to see anything save the bayoneting of a few wounded.

The blood down in the convent yard was steaming under the sun's rays. The last man of the Alamo was dead—one hundred and seventy of them; they had killed three times their number and had wounded as many more.

A Mexican officer led the women away from the church to San Antonio. Mrs. Dickinson got a horse in the town and rode to Gonzales with her baby. When the women and the old men who were left in the settlement heard her story they burned their houses behind them, that the enemy might find no plunder, and fled eastward.

On that Sunday, after the powder smoke lifted from the courtyard of the Alamo, a thicker smoke cloud rose to take its place. It rose in a straight column to the sky, as black as ink. By Santa Anna's orders the bodies of the men of Texas had been collected in a huge pile and were being burned. A few weeks later—after Sam Houston had defeated the dictator at San Jacinto—Captain Juan Seguin came back to the Alamo and found the ashes of his comrades. He gathered them up and gave them burial in a peach orchard near-by. The site of that grave is now forgotten.

In the old state house at Austin there stood

a monument. On each of its four sides it bore a name. Bowie, Bonham, Crockett and—on the front—Travis. Beneath this name there was a graven sentence:

THERMOPYLÆ HAD ITS MESSENGER OF DEFEAT. THE ALAMO HAD NONE.

WILLIAM BECKNELL

WILLIAM BECKNELL was a rover, weather-stained and hardened, one of that breed who sojourned on their clearings, tending their crops; but, when the longing came, fared forth in buckskin hunting-shirts and moccasins, with their powder-horns slung by their sides, and in their hands the long-barreled flint-lock rifles with which to get their meat and keep their scalps. In the summer of 1821 he was living at Boone's Lick, about one hundred and fifty miles up the Missouri from St. Louis.

Captain Becknell his neighbors called him—from the War of 1812, where he had served, and from two campaigns against the hostile Indians. They were a rough and ready lot, these neighbors; for the most part Kentuckians who had come into Howard county with the sons of Daniel Boone; there was a sprinkling of old-time Creole voyageurs who had brought back Indian wives from fur-

trading expeditions in the country of the Dakotas. Among them Becknell stood out as a
man of parts.

He was something of a scholar, and the
love of reading was strong in him. Now, as
he neared his middle age, the desire to settle
down was beginning to overmaster the longing for the wilderness. But the hard times
which had descended upon Missouri caught
him along with a good many others. That
paper-money panic which had so much to do
with the early pioneering of the country west
of the Mississippi put him in a position where
he had to mend his fortunes.

Right here it is worth while to pause and
note a fact ignored by histories. This hard-
times era which followed the War of 1812
was the direct cause of three business ven-
tures, all of which were conceived in Missouri, within one hundred and fifty miles of
St. Louis. By them this nation's conquest of
the West was assured. In this summer of 1821
William Ashley and Andrew Henry were
beginning the Rocky Mountain Fur Company, and Stephen Austin was founding his
land colony down on the Brazos River. From
these two projects—both of which were born

in the mining village of Potosi, Missouri—came the Overland Trail across the Rockies and the nation of Texas. Captain Becknell's attempt to rehabilitate himself resulted in the founding of the Santa Fé Trail.

But Santa Fé was not in Becknell's mind when he decided to take a final fling beyond the smell of other men's camp-fires. His idea was to make some money by trading with the Indians. It was in the town of Franklin that he stumbled on it.

The tawny Missouri booms along to-day over the spot where Franklin stood. It was a thriving place, with a tobacco factory and an academy; the point of departure for all the bold expeditions; the first sight of civilization for returning wanderers. Every spring the clumsy keel-boats tied up for a brief rest at the landing before resuming their slow journey up the coffee-colored river; trains of pack-mules with bulging *aparejoz* halted a little while, then filed away along the bank on their way to the southwestern prairies. And every fall, when the wild grapes were turning purple and the sumach was flaring crimson in the thickets, some weary, weather-worn rovers came straggling back to tell the tales of their wanderings. It was from one of these that Becknell got his idea.

The commodity on which this business venture hung was mules. Spanish mules from the Rio Grande and the valleys of Chihuahua. In those days the State of Missouri was already beginning to realize the value of the long-eared hybrids, for whose rearing she was to become famous in years to come. A good mule brought as high as seventy-five dollars in St. Louis then, and Becknell had learned of a market where you could buy one for two or three dollars' worth of gewgaws.

That market lay somewhere south of the headwaters of the Arkansas River—not far from where the boundaries of Colorado, Oklahoma and New Mexico now meet. If your luck was good you found it, and if your good luck hung on after finding it you kept your scalp and did your buying. For to this region the Comanches came across the Llano Estacado, after their raids on the Spanish presidios and haciendas to the southward. They came with fresh scalps dangling from their bridle reins, with herds of live-stock from a ravaged frontier. Hither, to meet them, came the comancheros—the Indian traders—from

Santa Fé and old Taos, and bartered with them for the loot. But the Spanish settlements were remote from markets, and the wares which these traders brought to the savages were of small inducement compared to St. Louis calicoes and beads. It was on these elements that Captain Becknell's business proposition hung.

The region where the Comanches came was practically unknown to Americans. Of those who had been there, only one or two had returned, and they had brought but little information. There was, moreover, a risk involved for any trader entering this *terra incognita*. For old Santa Fé, the City of the Holy Faith, lay sleeping down there in its valley under the Sangre de Cristo Mountains; and the intention of the Spanish authorities was that the sleep should continue, uninterrupted by any restless fortune-hunters from the raw young nation beyond the prairies. This was the reason why so few of those to go thither had come back to tell the story of the trail. The most of them had found their way to jails down in Chihuahua. But the element of risk, for the average Missourian of those days, lent enticing flavor to such an ex-

pedition as this. And when it came to lining
out a route, there happened to be a man near
Franklin who had traveled over most of the
ground.

Ezekiel Williams was his name, an old-
timer, and he lived at Arrow Rock, less than
a dozen miles from Becknell's home. In the
summer of 1809 he had left Manuel Lisa's
trading-post on the Yellowstone with a little
band of free trappers to wander southward
along the eastern slope of the Shining Mountains, which we call the Rockies now; and
the tale of his adventures, as he used to tell
it when he sat of evenings on the doorstep of
his cabin, would make the stories of old Ho-
mer's heroes seem tame by comparison. Some
of his company had gone as far as Santa Fé,
and he himself had spent several weeks in
the country about the headwaters of the Arkansas, to make his way homeward by the river
later on.

So Becknell went to Arrow Rock and had
more than one talk with old Ezekiel Williams; he watched the trapper draw maps in
the sand with a bit of stick; he learned the
route from these, according to the manner of
the Indians. And in the early summer of

1821 he set about organizing his expedition to trade gewgaws for mules with the Comanche Indians.

There was a weekly paper in the little town of Franklin, the westernmost journal in the United States. "The Missouri Intelligencer and the Boone's Lick Advertiser" was its name. On June 25, 1821, Becknell published an advertisement in its columns.

"An article for the government of a company of men destined to the westward for the purpose of trading horses and mules and catching wild animals of every description" —so it began. Equal shares and contributions from the members, every one of whom must bring his own horse, rifle and ammunition; these were the terms of subscription. Those who liked the idea were requested to meet at the home of Ezekiel Williams, five miles from Franklin—"where we will procure a pilot and appoint officers."

On the fourth of August seventeen men met at the old trapper's cabin by the Arrow Rock ferry. They elected Becknell as their leader and their guide. Within two weeks there was a second meeting at Franklin, and on the last day of the month the members rode to Williams's place, every man leading a pack-horse laden with such calicoes and beads and knick-knacks as he had been able to afford.

That evening the old-timer sat before his cabin door with a ring of sunburned adventurers around him. With a pointed stick he scratched faint lines upon the beaten earth.

"Here is a grove of hickory; the place where the three tribes come to smoke the pipe of peace . . . This is the Arkansas River . . . When ye've followed it for twelve or fourteen days into the west, the hills begin . . . Now ye are in the country of the Arapahoes—"

So he went on, and with the memory of those lines for their map they departed the next morning on their eight-hundred-mile journey. The little ferry took them across the muddy river. They went through the wooded bottom-lands; they climbed the bluffs and struck off southwest, over the rolling prairie.

A rainy autumn; they journeyed for three weeks through a cold gray downpour. Near where Topeka stands to-day they came to a wooded creek bottom called Council Grove, where the tribes of the Kansas prairies used to gather to renew their old treaties. Here they rested a day or two and killed wild turkeys; then traveled on southwest by the same route where express trains now thunder along at sixty miles an hour. They reached the Arkansas River and followed the valley up-stream to the west.

The prairie was as flat as a floor, as lonely as a sea; a circular expanse of dead grass, under the sky's huge bowl, bisected by the winding line of the river bottom, where the cottonwoods were turning gold and the wild-plum thickets showing scarlet tinges. They passed dog-towns; great herds of buffalo crossed their path, migrating southward, stretching from horizon to horizon. Bands of wild horses galloped off before them; and antelope glided away to melt into the horizon, silent as phantoms. By night the big lobo wolves gathered outside the circle of fire-light, peering at them through oblique eyes.

The river grew narrower and more rapid; the grass became scantier every day now. The horses were gaunt from lack of feed. On the fifteenth of October they came to a little lake near the Colorado boundary; they rested there three days, while the horses picked up strength from the feed about the shore, and the men made new moccasins. A week later, not far from where the town of La Junta, Colorado, stands to-day, they bore off to the southwest through bare grass hills to the mountains.

Here, somewhere close to the Raton Pass, by which the Santa Fé Railway crosses the range, they struggled up into the timber and on to rugged heights where only a few gnarled evergreens clung to the slopes, where flocks of mountain sheep looked down upon them from the ridges. They came to enormous boulder slides, the talus from sheer cliffs, and they toiled for two days removing the huge rocks to make a trail for their pack-horses. At last they gained the summit, where the wind cut them to the bone and the fresh snow fell on their blankets while they slept that night. Then they went downhill into the south and came to the gray oak-dotted mountains of northeastern New Mexico. The cold increased. There was no game. The horses swayed from weakness as they walked. This was where they had hoped to meet the Comanches; but there was no sign of Indians about. They had been gone from home for two months. Discouragement came over them, but they kept on.

They wandered back and forth for thirteen days. And still no sign. Eight hundred miles from home, their horses were worn out, the game had vanished; they felt the pinch of hunger. It began to look as if their expedition was a failure.

It was the morning of November 13. They had come down into the narrow valley where the Pecos River rises; a weary little cavalcade; sore-footed horses, hideously gaunt; the riders looked like bearded scarecrows. Through the scattered cottonwoods and pines some one caught sight of a party of approaching horsemen. Then dismay came upon them; these were Spanish cavalry. It seemed at that moment as if their bad luck had reached a climax. All those miles of weariness and hardship were to end apparently—as they had ended with more than one trading outfit before—in a Mexican jail.

But when the swarthy troopers, with their huge spurs and flaring breeches faced with leather, drew up, the officer in charge approached Becknell with outstretched hand. To the Missourians his words were unintelligible; but his smile was unmistakable. It was quite evident that for the present at least they were not under arrest.

No man in either party knew the other party's language, but they managed to communicate by signs. When the commanding officer ordered some of the men to prepare a meal, his half-famished guests began to suspect that something must have happened out in this part of the world to change the governmental attitude toward strangers. The two outfits spent that night in camp together, and the next day the soldiers took them to the village of San Miguel—some fifty miles or so from Santa Fé.

As the Missourians rode up the narrow street of San Miguel the people came out from the flat-roofed adobe houses and flocked around them. Their faces were smiling. "Los Americanos," they cried. There was a Frenchman in the place who had found his way hither from the City of Mexico some years before. He knew a few words of English and Becknell knew a little of the Creole French as it was spoken in the country near St. Louis. These two sat down together in the plaza and Becknell learned the reason for this unexpected demonstration. Mexico had seceded from Spain. The days of the captains-general were gone and the bars were down for American traders.

Instead of finding the Comanches and their Spanish mules, he had stumbled on a new market, whose silver dollars were to lure trains of wagons across the prairies for more than twenty years to come.

The next morning Becknell and his companions set out for Santa Fé, with the Frenchman as their interpreter. Two days later the little pack-train came to a halt in the sandy plaza from whose four sides the narrow crooked streets radiated to all parts of the City of the Holy Faith. Now every one of those streets began disgorging crowds into the barren square: fat señoras clad in black from head to foot; lithe señoritas with their dark eyes glowing eagerly from beneath the rebozos; caballeros in slashed velvet breeches, their spurs making faint music on the dry earth. The packs were opened and their contents spread out on blankets; the buyers gathered round the ragged, weather-stained merchants. And on that afternoon common calicoes, which had cost twenty cents a yard in St. Louis, went for as high as three dollars a yard.

A day or two later, by invitation, Becknell visited the governor in the long one-story palace which fronted the dusty plaza. His host asked him a hundred questions concerning the United States, and voiced the hope that, in the years to come, the trail from Missouri to Santa Fé would be traveled by many wagon trains.

Early in February William Becknell came back to Franklin with a few half-healed frostbites for souvenirs of his winter journey across the plains, with a good-sized sack of Mexican dollars, and with that idea, suggested by the governor, of a wagon train to Santa Fé. During the early spring he set to work to raise five thousand dollars and another company of traders.

On the twenty-second of May three covered wagon lumbered down the Missouri's bank to the Arrow Rock ferry. Six mules to a team; the clumsy vehicles were loaded down with calicoes and knickknacks from St. Louis. Twenty-one men in the company; the most of them were in the saddle. The little flatboat made a dozen trips to take them across the river. The caravan entered the woods on the other side and passed from sight. The wagon trade to Santa Fé—the commerce of the prairies—was begun.

They traveled into the Southwest, leaving the first wheel tracks on the tough Kansas sod, to mark the route which steel rails were to span in after-years. One night a herd of buffalo stampeded twenty of their horses. While searching for the animals two of the company were captured by Osage Indians, who flogged them and stripped them of their possessions. They lost eight days in recovering the plunder from the savages and rounding up the stampeded stock. So it was past the middle of June when they left the valley of the Arkansas, fifty miles or so from where Dodge City stands to-day, and struck out for the valley of the Cimmaron.

This new route was a short cut to Santa Fé and it avoided the rugged heights of the Raton Pass. Some of the New Mexican comancheros had told Becknell about it. An unmarked trail. You crossed the Divide between the two rivers, and when you found the Cimmaron you followed it up through what is now western Oklahoma, to its headwaters.

There was, however, an essential fact which was not included in Becknell's information— in the dry weather the Cimmaron seeps underground; its bed is a sun-baked arroyo.

So they started on that long dry drive of sixty-odd miles without any water save what they carried in their canteens. At first their road lay through a sand-hill country. They eased the covered wagons down into deep gullies; they doubled the mule-teams to pull them up the steep-cut banks. There were miles of side-hill-going where it often took half the company to keep a wagon from capsizing. A hot day; the mules were reeking with sweat; the men were drinking deep from their canteens before noontime. They gained the summit of the last rise and came out on the forty-mile plateau which separates the Arkansas from the Cimmaron.

The sun had baked the earth as dry as ashes. The prickly-pear sprawled all about; there were a few low bitter weeds, whose leaves fell into powder at the touch. The dust rose from the hoofs of the plodding mules and from the wagon-wheels in thick clouds; it settled down upon the men and animals in a gray film. The arid land was as level as a floor;

the sky was like a brazen bowl made hideous by the sun's malevolence.

They plodded on, keeping to the southwest. The mules were gaunt with thirst; some of the men who had used up their store were begging water of their fellows. That night they dry-camped.

The sun came up above the rigid circle of the horizon like a big ball of fire the next morning. The mules were half-crazed from thirst; the men had to fight them to get the harness on them. They struck out—a line of dark dots on the surface of a flat gray circle —under a dome of glaring brass. That morning they drank the last water from the canteens.

Some time during this second day they thought they saw a lake; and as they looked the waters rippled; the green trees moved gently in a breeze. The teamsters, who had been sitting silent, shouted aloud and whipped up their mules. The riders spurred their jaded horses. But when they approached, the vision rose into the air and vanished, leaving a bare white expanse of alkali where it had been. They had been looking at a phantom. They resumed their journey, uncomprehending, smitten with the mystery. And, as they traveled through the long hours, new mirages appeared beside their path to mock them.

Save where the passing buffalo had gouged out a wallow, or left their shallow winding trails, the land was like a floor. The skeletons of a few bison lay among the sprawling prickly-pear. The dust clouds hung over the caravan, and the reddened eyes of the men smarted as with acrid smoke. Their lips were cracked and bleeding. That night they made another dry camp.

The next day the tongues of some of them began to swell. And some began to see strange things. The little gray shrubs which had been so stiff and still seemed to be moving. They swelled into enormous size and took the shapes of animals. The country ahead was growing broken; the hills of sand seemed to be gliding back and forth in a grotesque slow dance.

They traveled on through the sand-hills. Some of the men were so weak with thirst that they were unable to raise a hand in work. The stronger ones had double toil, easing the clumsy wagons down the steeper pitches. But they buoyed themselves up by the thought that this was the downhill pull—somewhere ahead the Cimmaron lay near-by now.

When they came down into the valley they found a wide wash; its bed was dry; the loose sand rose in clouds of thin dust about the wagon-wheels; the rocks lay stark in the hot sunshine. Instead of a river, they had attained desolation. Now some of them were babbling in thirst's delirium; and some were sitting with bowed heads staring before them with unseeing eyes; the tongues of some were black and swollen, thrust between their lips.

They never dreamed that the stream was seeping beneath their feet. They forced their mules up the bank and toiled on, hoping to find the river over the next rise.

They struggled up-grade through hills of shifting sand, and when they gained the first benchland one of the drivers uttered a croaking cry. A pond of water showed a mile or so ahead. But, as they neared it, it rose into the air and vanished. The mirage had deceived them again. That afternoon they killed their dogs and drank the hot blood; but instead of relieving their torture it turned them deathly sick.

Now those of them who were able to reason gathered in council. The country rose before them to another high plateau. Either they had missed their way or the Cimmaron was a myth, so they told each other. Their only hope of living was to go back to the Arkansas. Without water they could never live the distance through.

Then, when despair was settling down upon them, one of the men pointed down the arid slopes which they had climbed. A form was coming out of the dry wash. Their eyes had become so used to phantoms, born of sun-glare and heat-waves, that for some time they were not sure whether this was reality or some new specter. It came on slowly and they saw it was a buffalo.

A solitary old bull, driven away from some herd to end his days alone. His mane was matted and his flanks were lean. They would have passed him by with scorn on a hunt; but they were hoping for something more precious than meat now. Somewhere down there he must have found a water-hole and drunk his fill.

Several of the men took their rifles and crept out on their bellies to intercept him. When he was not more than one hundred yards away, they fired. He staggered forward

and his knees doubled under him; he sank
down dying.

They ripped the body open. The stomach
was distended. They drained the tepid fluid
out. There were several swallows for every
man. In after years one of the company told
Josiah Gregg, who wrote "The Commerce
of the Prairies," that nothing ever passed his
lips which gave him such exquisite delight
as that filthy draft.

Now two of the stronger ones took an arm-
ful of canteens apiece and followed the animal's fresh trail back into the wash. When
they had traveled several miles they found
a tepid pool in the sand. They brought the
filled canteens to their companions, and by
evening the others had revived enough to
take the wagons to the water-hole.

By this time Becknell understood the situation. They were not lost. This was the valley
of the Cimmaron; the river lay buried in the
sand; they followed the dry bed into the west.
Some days they came to pools, and sometimes
they dug into the hot earth to find the water.
Three weeks after they had come down into
the valley they reached its head in north-

eastern New Mexico and crossed a divide to Rock Creek, a tributary of the Canadian. Their way was blocked by high limestone cliffs. They took their wagons apart and carried up the pieces on their backs one at a time. They snubbed the mules up to the summit; put the vehicles together and went on.

One day in the middle of the summer they came into the valley at the foot of the Sangre de Cristo range, where the old city of Santa Fé had lain sleeping for so many years. And, as the clumsy wagons with their dust-stained and tattered canvas covers rattled into the sandy plaza, the narrow streets became alive with people. Caballeros, trapped out in velvet, with little silver ornaments tinkling on the wide rims of their sombreros; brown-robed priests; ladies with lace scarfs and dainty fans; officials from the palace of the governor; wood-sellers from the mountains with their laden burros; crippled beggars; and dogs everywhere.

The gaunted mules were unhitched; some of them rolled luxuriously in the loose sand and others woke the echoes with their discordant braying. The shouts of the crowd grew louder—

"Los Americanos!" "Los Caros!" "La entrada de la caravan!"

The bearded, weather-stained men of Missouri unpacked their wares for eager buyers, who paid more than ten times the St. Louis prices. And that autumn William Becknell returned to Franklin with another sack of Mexican dollars.

Now Franklin became the point of departure for many wagon trains to Santa Fé. Later on, the new town of Independence got the business. And during the next twenty years the trail whose first wheel tracks had been made by Becknell's wagons became the highway for an enormous commerce. The restless people of Missouri and the Ohio Valley began to make their way into the remote places of the Southwest—and on to California.

JAMES PATTIE

I T was spring when James Pattie and his father left the log cabin and the sawmill on the wooded banks of the Gasconade River. The two were footloose, with no ties to bind them; for death had come to the cabin that winter; and when Sylvester Pattie buried his wife he sickened at the sight of the familiar things. So he sold the land, turned the rest of the children over to relatives and took the long-barreled rifle with which he had fought his way hither from the Kentucky hills, to leave Missouri with his eldest son and forget his sorrow in the hard excitement of the wilderness.

They journeyed to St. Louis, one hundred miles away. The town was humming like a hive of bees. A thousand men bent on a hundred mighty quests were making their rendezvous here. Big-boned flatboat men who had followed the ice down the Ohio gathered on the river bank to talk, in a jargon of Creole French, bastard Spanish and backwoods English, of voyages down the Mississippi to distant Natchez and New Orleans. Groups of French Canadian voyageurs from Mackinaw, in their party-colored blanket coats and their scarlet sashes, chattered in the sunshine with swarthy half-breed *courriers des bois,* scarcely distinguishable from the silent sloe-eyed Indians who lounged beside them, while they bided the loading of the fur company's keelboats for the summer's expedition to the head of the distant Yellowstone. Uptown the noises of building mingled with the rattle of heavy wagons and two-wheeled carts. Here and there among the new brick walls there remained a white mansion with long French windows and wide verandas; and now and then a goateed Frenchman, with his wide hat, ruffled shirt and tight-strapped trousers, passed among the crowds that thronged the wooden sidewalks. Occasionally there came some of those lean, weather-beaten men in butternut jeans and deerskin hunting-shirts who had pressed onward from Virginia to Kentucky, and from Kentucky through the Ohio forests, seeking this outlet to a new frontier. Sylvester Pattie hailed more than one of them to talk of the recent War of 1812, when he had led a company of them against the allied tribes.

Sometimes the two new-comers saw gaunt savage men whose beards were shot with gray, whose skin the sun and wind had burned as red as any Indian's, whose hair hung to the shoulders beneath great caps of foxskin. Their garments of smoke-tanned buckskin were fringed with colored porcupine quills; their moccasins were ornate with patterned beads; the stocks of their long-barreled rifles and their powder-horns were decorated with brass tacks. Their deep-set eyes held the same steadiness which some of us of a later generation have seen in the eyes of old prospectors. These were free trappers who had wandered across the prairies and the sage-brush hills to rove among the solitudes of the snow peaks which part the waters of the continent.

In St. Louis the father made up his mind to go into the country of the upper Missouri. He bought supplies: salt, coffee, flour, tobacco, traps, powder, lead. He outfitted with goods for trading with the Indians: bright-colored cloth, tomahawks, knives, beads and gewgaws. He found three followers, loaded the bulk of his stores on a keel-boat, which was to take the stuff as far as Council Bluffs; from there the little company started on horseback, following the river's course.

They journeyed through the woodlands past the last fringe of cabins where Creole trappers lived with their Indian wives and broods of dusky children; they reached the edge of the prairies; and at Cabanne's trading-post, where Omaha now stands, they fell in with Sylvester Pratte, son of a famous fur trader, who was about to leave for Santa Fé with a large pack-train. He needed a veteran to handle his expedition and he tried to persuade Pattie to join him; but the Missourian shook his head. He was set on seeing the upper Missouri.

However, when the Patties reached the military post at Council Bluffs the commandant informed them that they could not traffic with the Indians in the upper country without a permit. Summer was well along. Rather than lose the time to go back to St. Louis and obtain official permission, the father decided to change his plans.

"We'll go to Santa Fé," he said, "with Pratte."

They struck off westward across the prairie

for the banks of the main Platte. Three or four evenings later they came down into the cottonwoods and willows by the river bottom where the camp-fires were twinkling among the trees. The Pratte party numbered more than one hundred men, Missourians for the most part; and when they saw Sylvester Pattie, who had gained fame in the War of 1812 as captain of a company of rangers, they swung their wide-rimmed hats and cheered. It was agreed that night that he should take command. A few days later they lined out on the old trapper's trail—very much the same route as Lieutenant Zebulon Pike had taken—by way of the Platte and the eastern fringes of the Rocky Mountains for Santa Fé.

Three hundred pack-mules, one hundred and sixteen men mounted on saddle horses; that was the caravan. Outriders kept well ahead, and far on either side were seasoned backwoodsmen, bearing their long-barreled muzzle rifles across their saddle bows. Within this thin fringe of scouts the mules lined out behind a white bell-mare, flanked by the other members of the company. About them all the green prairie stretched away as level as the sea.

On the first evening they reached a friendly village of the Pawnee Loups just as a party of young warriors was returning from an expedition against the distant Comanches with half a dozen scalps and a little boy whom they had taken prisoner. When darkness came the war-drums boomed and all the braves joined in a scalp dance. For three days and nights they leaped about the pole upon which the bloody trophies hung. The captive lay, half-dead from thirst and hunger, in a lodge nearby. At last the ceremonial reached a climax and the naked warriors surged yelling to the tepee to bring the child forth for the torture. They found Sylvester Pattie and his son in the doorway; the open space about was filled with the Missouri backwoodsmen.

"I'll give ten yards of broadcloth for the boy," the elder Pattie told them and unrolled a bolt of scarlet fabric before the chief. The latter shook his head.

"All right," said Pattie, "we'll take him anyhow." The Indian looked about him at the circle of white men with their rifles in their hands.

"Do you think," he asked slowly, "that you can do it?"

"If we should die," Pattie answered, "our countrymen will come and destroy your nation."

The chief considered for a moment.

"Throw in a paper of vermilion, then," he said.

So when the company departed from the village the youngster rode behind the saddle of a bearded rifleman, and in the evenings he played among the dogs about the camp-fire.

They left the prairies and came out on the great plains where the earth was baked to rocklike hardness by the summer sun. They saw the passing herds of buffalo. One night the report of a sentry's rifle brought them leaping from their blankets and they fought off a band of prowling Arickarees who had sought to steal their horses. They reached the prairie-dog villages and the rolling uplands. They turned into the southwest, and when they were crossing the low cut-bank hills between the headwaters of the Republican and the Smoky Hill they found the stark bodies of two white men lying asprawl in the afternoon sunshine. A multitude of horse tracks and five dead Crow Indians near-by told the story of the fight. Young James Pattie and ten others followed the trail of the savages to their camp. That night sixty men surrounded the place, and when the Crows rolled out of their blankets in the dawn the long-barreled rifles flashed behind the rocks and sage-brush clumps until the camp became a shambles, with thirty bodies among the ashes of the fires.

September came. The hills grew higher. The expedition ran out of salt and flour. In a little draw where the juniper and bull pine grew they fell in with a band of wandering Comanches, whom they coaxed into their camp to do some trading. A warrior caught sight of the Indian boy, who was playing about the fire, and his yell of joy brought his companions to his side. White men and red watched him press the youngster to his bosom. It was his son.

The pack-train wound its way into the mountains. One night a grizzly-bear stole into camp and killed a horse. He turned upon the

men and wounded one so badly that they had
to leave him with two companions to wait
for him to die.

Early in November they came down into
the valley of the Taos; and when they had
paid duty on their goods to the alcalde of the
old pueblo they journeyed on to Santa Fé.

The City of the Holy Faith lay drowsing
by the headwaters of the Rio Grande, surrounded by pallid mountains. Dogs swarmed
in all the narrow streets. Women whose faces
were almost hidden by the tightly drawn rebozos stared at the ragged-bearded horsemen
and the laden pack-mules. Sombreroed men,
with picturesque serapes and leather breeches
slashed open from the knees, slouched along
after the cavalcade, to lounge at ease in the
wide plaza before the governor's one-story
palace, watching the unloading of the packs.
The arrival of Americans was a rare thing in
those days, and not a family in the place but
was eager to buy some of the wares from
distant St. Louis.

But Sylvester Pattie had talked with his
son of richer opportunities than trade, and now
the project of getting beaver skins in the unknown land beyond the crests of the pallid

mountains was uppermost in both their minds.
Some one had told them of the Gila River.
They went to the one-story palace with its wide
verandas and asked Governor Bartolomé Baca
for a permit to trap and trade along the stream.

He hemmed and hawed. They offered him
5 per cent of their catch. Still he delayed
decision. It began to look as if they were going to meet with refusal. But one night a
horseman rode into town with news that the
Mescalero Apaches had raided the settlements in the upper Pecos Valley and carried
off five women, among whom was the daughter
of a former Spanish governor. Four hundred
cavalry were lined up in the plaza the next
morning to go forth against the savages. Sylvester Pattie saw his opportunity. He volun-
teered to take his backwoodsmen with the
expedition. The officer in charge went him
one better and gave him the command.

So the Mexican cavalry clattered away
from Santa Fé that morning with one hundred lean, sunbrowned Missourians riding in
the van. Three days later they picked up the
trail of the Apaches somewhere near where
Fort Sumner afterward stood. They traveled
hard into the southwest for two nights and

days and on the third morning, as they were approaching El Capitan Mountains, the scouts came back to the main body with tidings that they had sighted the Indians hurrying up a canyon toward the summit of the range.

"I'll take my men by a roundabout course to the head of the pass," Sylvester Pattie told the Mexican commander, "and ambush them there. You follow them up the gulch and, when you hear our firing, close in."

An hour later young James Pattie lay on his belly behind a rock in the little swale where the pass crossed the summit, and listened to the orders which his father gave the men about him.

"They'll kill those women if they get the chance," the old Indian-fighter said. "We mustn't give them time for that. As soon as they show up, you on the right flank give them a volley. While you're reloading, the left of the line will keep up a running fire."

Time passed. There came the sound of hoof-beats. A band of horses appeared trotting up the narrow gulch; a drove of sheep followed them in the canyon bed. The watchers saw the herders—five white women, half-naked, panting with the hard climb. Half a dozen turbaned Apaches rode close behind them with lances in their hands.

The men behind the rocks remained as still as the earth on which they lay. There was no sound except the thudding of the hoofs and the plaintive voices of the sheep. Just as the canyon was filling with Indian warriors a horse in the lead of the herd got scent of the ambush and shied off up the hillside. The frowsy-haired riders behind the women glanced sharply toward the spot. The long-barreled rifles united in a crashing chorus. The narrow gulch became a thick confusion of plunging horses; the sheep milled in piti-ful, bleating panic; turbaned brown bodies slid limply from the ponies' backs to vanish in the dust clouds among the trampling hoofs.

The women emerged from the dust haze and ran toward the ambuscade. Several Apache horsemen dashed along the hillside after them. Their lances flashed in the hot sunshine, rising above the ponies' uptossed manes.

Young Pattie leaped from his cover, swing-ing his clubbed rifle above his head. A dozen others were at his heels. A man beside him fell dead. He saw three of the captives sink to the earth, transfixed by lances. The two surviving women were striving toward him, with a naked savage close behind. The warrior's lean brown arm flew upward; the spear hung for an instant poised above the foremost of the fugitives. The weapon started to descend; it faltered and went wild, and the Indian pitched forward with a bullet between his eyes. A moment later the two women fell half-fainting at young Pattie's feet.

They took the rescued pair back to the line; then fell upon their knees and went to reloading their rifles. While they crouched behind their cover, firing at every turbaned head that showed, there rose a murmur among the Missourians.

"Where are those Mexicans?" they asked one another.

At last the Indians began falling back. As the white men followed them, creeping from rock to rock, they heard a volley in the gulch below them. But the Mexican troops fled as soon as they had discharged their pieces, and the Apaches rallied where the canyon opened out. They turned on the Americans so fiercely that it seemed for a few minutes as if they would carry everything before them. Finally they broke and ran. And then the Mexican soldiers came eagerly to massacre the wounded. Sylvester Pattie drove them off, and there were high words between him and the Spanish commander, who took his men back to Santa Fé, leaving the Americans to follow by themselves.

During that march they learned that one of the women who had fallen at young James Pattie's feet was the daughter of the former Spanish governor. And when they reached the capital the elder Pattie was able to gain his coveted permission to go after beaver down the Gila. Within a week the Missourians had split into numerous small parties bent on trading and trapping.

One hundred and sixteen of them when they started from the Platte; now there were less than one hundred living, and a year later there remained only sixteen. Sickness and savages and the grim southwestern wilderness got all the rest.

It was at the beginning of the winter of 1824-25 when young James Pattie went with his father and five men down the Rio Grande to Socorro, thence across the mountains toward the headwaters of the Gila River, where no American had set foot before. That was a winter of great adventures all along the backbone of the Continental Divide. Far to the north a young fellow of the name of Jedediah Smith was holed up on the headwaters of the Snake River, making his plans for the extension of the Rocky Mountain Fur Company, which plans were subsequently to take him across the passes of the Sierra Nevada Mountains. Jim Bridger, still a boy in years, was trapping beaver along the streams which he was to follow before the next spring to the spot where the mountains widened and gave him the view of the Great Salt Lake. Other lean, weather-stained sons of Kentucky and Tennessee were prowling along the watercourses which led upward toward the fields of perpetual snow, dodging Indians, eating their saddle horses sometimes when game was scarce. Up on the Sweetwater one of these men named Scott, left dying by his companions, crawled sixty miles on hands and knees before he gave up to death. And Peg Leg Smith, with his leg broken and no man to help him, amputated the limb himself in a cabin among the Wasatch Mountains.

These were the free trappers. Young James Pattie was now one of them. He rode with his companions into the unknown wilderness, a typical specimen of those pathfinders whose part in their country's history the text-books of our schools have studiously ignored—a roll of blankets behind his saddle cantle; in front on ·either side a bunch of beaver traps; in his right hand, and held athwart the saddle bow, the long eight-square muzzle-loading flintlock rifle. He wore a cap of foxskin under which his hair hung to his shoulders; a loose hunting-coat and fringed breeches of smoke-tanned buckskin; and he was shod in moccasins. A powder-horn hung by his side, and in his belt there were two pistols and a butcher knife.

Somewhere among the hills they fell in with seven other American trappers and the two parties joined forces. At the Santa Rita copper mines, which the Mexicans were then working, they rested their horses, and early in December they went on, over ridges and up canyons, until they reached the Gila's headwaters. Hunting was good. They found beaver signs and split into pairs to work the different streams. James Pattie went with a companion following a mountain creek, wading waist deep sometimes to set their traps, sleeping by night beneath the snapping stars. When they returned to the others they learned that the seven who had joined forces with them had deserted. Now the party followed the Gila westward, but the seceders had trapped the country clean ahead of them and frightened off the game. Lean days came; their horses went sore-footed. Finally they reached the mouth of the San Francisco and got good hunting. While they were here six of the deserters came into their camp and told how the Indians had stolen their horses, killing one of their number. They begged three ponies and enough provisions to reach the copper mines.

The Patties continued westward, until a band of Indians ambushed them somewhere in the southern slope of the White Mountains and ran off most of their horses after an ugly battle.

For three months after that they wandered back and forth along the streams. They climbed into the deep snows; they came down into the long open mesas where the giant cactus forests grew. Sometimes they slept without

camp-fires for fear of prowling savages.
There were days when they were glad to get
a stray raven or a buzzard for food. They
staggered on, with their moccasins worn out
and their feet bleeding, reeling from hunger's
weakness, until they were back to the San
Francisco River and got meat again. They
cached their furs and returned to the Santa
Rita mines.

Now Sylvester Pattie was beginning to feel
that he had had enough of trapping and he
took a lease of the mines. But the boy was
still on fire, and in the spring he joined a
party of twelve French Canadian trappers.
They went down the Gila, through the arid
deserts, to its mouth. They traded with the
naked Yumas on the banks of the turgid Colorado. They turned into the north, and somewhere near the mouth of Bill Williams Fork
they had a bloody battle with a bunch of
Mojave Indians who tried to steal their
horses.

They followed the rim of the Grand Canyon, and cursed the cliffs to admire which
men now travel across the continent; for they
could not reach the stream bed, and there
were no beaver on these arid table-lands. They

saw the Hopi villages on their lofty mesas;
they trafficked with the Navajos along the
San Juan. They journeyed north to the Wind
River country, where, in what is now Wyoming, they fought a fierce battle against the
Shoshones. They wandered farther on to the
banks of the distant Yellowstone. They crossed
the mountains to the upper Snake; then re-
crossed and came back southward along the
foothills, past the upper Platte, the Arkansas
and the Cimarron until at last they saw the
flat roofs of Santa Fé down in the sunshiny
valley before them.

Their pack-horses were laden with beaver
pelts. But while they were in the first flush
of joy at reaching the city the governor sent
for them.

"Where is your permit to trap and trade?"
he demanded.

James Pattie showed him the one which
had been issued after that battle with the
Mescalero Apaches.

"That has run out," the governor said, and
bade the soldiers confiscate the furs.

So young Pattie rode over the mountains
to the copper mines of Santa Rita with noth-

ing more than a tale of hard luck to show for all his months in the wilderness.

"Better," his father told him, "you settle down here with me. We can make good money." The young fellow tried it—but the occasional brushes with the Apaches and the grizzly-bear hunts were too tame for him. He took a trip into old Mexico and saw strange things. Returning in the summer of 1827, he learned that a bookkeeper had absconded with all the profits of the mines.

"We'll go on down the Gila," the father said, "and we'll strike out from its mouth to California."

They outfitted in Santa Fé; and on the eve of their departure they fell in with thirty trappers bound on a similar venture. Sylvester Pattie managed to get a permit for the whole party to trap and trade. In part because of this and in part because of his experience at Indian-fighting they chose him for their leader.

So on September 23, 1827, they set forth from the City of the Holy Faith. Probably they foresaw some of the obstacles which lay before them; but they did not even dream of certain surprises which Nature held in store beyond the western skyline.

Right at the outset Sylvester Pattie made a rule whereby the man who deserted or refused to obey orders was to be shot. Before they had been a week in the mountains by the Gila's headwaters they began to realize the necessity for this grim law; for game was scarce; they had to eat their dogs; they had some ugly Indian-fighting, and it took iron discipline to hold them all together. They traveled on westward into the long dry plains where the giant cactus grew. There famine came again; they killed some of their saddle horses and picked the bones clean. One day late in November, when they were down below the Maricopa flats, all but eight of the company deserted and struck off toward the mountains in the northwest. What became of them remains one of the desert's many mysteries.

The others kept on. Within a week they reached the Gila's mouth and found a village of Yuma Indians upon the Colorado's eastern bank. It was past noon. The naked warriors came forth from their tule lodges and gathered about the little group of white men.

James Pattie and his father talked with them in the silent sign language which was universal among the western tribes. Some of the older savages said that there were Christian settlements farther down the stream. They may have meant the Mexican seaports on the Gulf of California; they may have lied. At any rate, they told the story and in time it bore its fruit.

While they were holding this conference Sylvester Pattie was keeping one eye on the strapping warriors in the crowd about them; and what he saw he did not like.

"There are too many of these Indians," he told his followers. "Better we cross the river and make our camp on the other side."

So they swam their horses over and set about preparations to make down their beds; but before they were fairly at it, there came two hundred bucks, as naked as the day they were born, some of them swimming and some in frail canoes.

"Pack up and move, boys," said Sylvester Pattie. They loaded the tired horses once more and struck off up-stream for sixteen miles. It was nearly dark when the leader thought it wise to stop; and they had no time

to build a corral for the ponies, which was
their usual custom among hostile Indians. Before they had the camp-fire fairly started it
began to rain. The night came down black
dark. The storm grew harder. The thunder
cracked; the lightning flashed. They heard
the picketed horses snorting in the tules. And
as they were looking toward the spot, there
came a terrific peal of thunder. Silence followed. Then there rose on all sides of them
the hideous shrill war-whoop. The trappers
ran to save the ponies and found only the
severed picket ropes.

"We'll build canoes," Sylvester Pattie proposed, "and go on down the river to those
settlements."

They made a barricade of logs to fortify
their camp and they kept a sentry posted in a
tree-top, while the others went to work cutting down cottonwoods. They hollowed out
eight clumsy little boats, loaded in their
furs and started paddling down the Colorado.

At first they took it slowly, trapping as they
went, but as the days went on they noticed that
the pelts of the beaver were growing poorer
in this warm climate. So they contented them-

selves with what they had; it was a large catch—enough to make every man of them comfortable for the rest of his days, provided they ever got it back to market.

The Yumas dogged their course, seeking to ambush them when they came close to the banks. There came a time when the river seemed to be running along the summit of a ridge, and they could look out from their little crafts upon bottomlands that lay below them. They passed this seeming miracle; but a few evenings later they were confronted by another.

They had gone ashore and made their camp in the flat beside the great tawny flood. They did not know that they were within a few miles of its mouth; and had they known it, they would never have dreamed of the phenomenon which was about to take place; for they were inland men, ignorant of the ways of the sea. Darkness came down. They rolled up in their blankets.

As they lay there, they heard a faint murmur; it grew and grew until it was like the rushing of a wind among the branches. A man shouted in alarm. The water had climbed the bank and was creeping into his bed.

The others leaped from their blankets. One lighted a torch. They saw a brown wave marching straight up-stream toward them. They seized their canoes and a few minutes later were paddling over the spot where their camp had been, rescuing such bits of flotsam as they could lay their hands on.

The hours went by. The waters began to recede. Dawn came and the earth lay bare again. They spent a hard morning recovering their beaver pelts and supplies, and young Pattie, who had been down to Guaymas the year before, remembered how he had seen the tides come in. So that explained the miracle. But the explanation left them confronting a new problem. Their cranky little canoes would never weather such swells as this. Farther travel into the southward was impossible and they could not make good progress up-stream against the current.

They were afoot; eight men in the heart of the southwestern deserts surrounded by hostile savages.

"We can buy horses on the seacoast," the Patties told the others. "Then we can return, pick up the pelts and go on back to Santa Fé."

So they decided to cache their furs and walk to California.

They traveled up-stream for ten miles or so, and there they buried the beaver pelts after the manner of the trappers, lining the pit with skins, removing all the superfluous earth and throwing it into the river; and finally covering the hole with the original layer of leaf mold. When they had every twig and stone in place, making the surface look as if it had been untouched, they took some dried beaver meat, their rifles, blankets and ammunition and struck off across the bottomlands into the west.

On the second day they emerged from the tangle of vines and brush and came up into low sandhills. They climbed the ridges and the sun was growing hot. They passed on to a salt plain that glistened white as snow.

They toiled westward straight into the hottest, driest desert of North America. Since their day many men have made that journey across the peninsula of Baja California, but few came forth without a memory of grim hardship that lasted as long as they lived. And more than one left his bones to dry beneath that scorching sun.

The long plain seemed to lengthen as they went. Their skins grew fevered, their tongues began to swell with thirst; the mirage rose before them and they staggered toward the phantom waters, to see the vision dissolve into the glaring sky. That night they flung themselves upon the scorched earth and slept. In the morning the sun flayed them again.

Low hills appeared ahead. They reached the range and climbed through loose earth above their ankles. They struggled on in single file, and young Pattie always held the lead. At last he gained the summit of a ridge and saw real waters shimmering below him in the sunshine. He waved his hand. The others hurried after him. But when they reached the shore they found the water bitter brine.

The long lake lay between them and the west. The Pacific Ocean and the Spanish settlements were over there somewhere beyond the horizon. They took their butcher knives and cut great bundles of the tules which grew about the edges of the sink; they lashed the bundles together into rafts and placed their packs upon them. Then they swam and waded, pushing the rafts before them; and when they reached the other side they struck out into the desert.

Within a mile James Pattie saw the tracks of Indians. They followed these and reached a beaten trail. They hung to it and staggered up a little draw which led them into a range of stucco mountains. At last they beheld the smoke of camp-fires.

These might be the fires of hostile savages. They did not know. Nor did they care. As well to die by arrows as to perish of thirst. They plodded on across the next summit and saw the lodges of considerable villages by a living stream.

The inhabitants fled at the sight of these ragged-bearded men. They lay behind the ridges and watched them fall upon their bellies by the ice-cold creek. Then some of them came stealing back, to make their peace with the wanderers and give them food.

A few days later the eight trappers set forth again into the west. One of the Indians went with them as their guide. Across the range of mountains, he said, were white men; but the trail was steep and there was no water for many miles.

They climbed under a savage sun. The dry
air seemed to sear their lungs. Their water
ran out. Thirst returned to torture them. The
naked Indian walked on before, and when
the weaker ones of the company began to lag
he exhorted them by signs to keep on. What
they had endured during the first stage of
their journey from the Colorado was as nothing compared to the punishment which Nature gave them now. Night yielded a little
surcease; and then the blazing day came back.
Their tongues turned black and protruded
from their mouths. They could not speak. The
Indian pointed on ahead. They did their best
to stumble after him. James Pattie saw his
father and another man sink down. He left
them lying there and crawled up the arid
canyon, on his bleeding hands and knees. At
last he reached the head of the gorge and
found a limpid stream emerging from the
rocks, to bury itself within a few yards in the
hot sand. He filled his powder-horn with
water as soon as he was able to travel and
brought it to the pair who had lain down to
die.

They rested for some hours and crossed the
summit of the range. They came down the

western slope to the mission of Santa Cata-
lina on the headwaters of the San Quentin
River. And when they stumbled into the quad-
rangle among the rambling adobe buildings
before the church, footsore, gaunt with hunger
and weary from their long hardships, they
got their first inkling of the trick which Fate
had prepared for them.

Some months before, the viceroy had sent
word from the City of Mexico to arrest all
Americans without passports. There was a
general fear of filibusters in the Spanish possessions. And when the Dominican fathers
saw this new band of tattered, weather-stained
adventurers and heard their wild tale, they
did what they deemed to be the prudent thing.

The Patties had come all these weary
leagues and suffered all these hardships—only
to land in jail.

The prisoners were sent to San Diego. Governor Echeandia of California listened to the
tale which James Pattie and his father told.
They showed him the permit from the governor at Santa Fé to trap and trade.

"That is worthless in California," he said;
and, to the officer in charge: "Put them behind
the bars."

The weeks dragged by. The hardships which he had undergone had left Sylvester Pattie worn out: jail life brought on his last sickness. He died alone in his cell; and his son, by special dispensation of the governor, was allowed to witness the burial.

More weary months followed. Through the intervention of Captain Cunningham and Captain John Bradshaw, two Yankee skippers whose ships were in San Diego Harbor, James Pattie was finally given a little more liberty. Sometimes he served as interpreter for the authorities; and finally he secured from Echeandia an agreement whereby the other luckless members of the expedition were to return to the Colorado with pack-horses to recover the cached beaver pelts. If they could produce the skins, the governor said, he would believe their contention that they were honest trappers and set them free. But when the party reached the spot, they found that a great freshet had washed out a new river channel. The furs were gone. Echeandia clapped them all into jail again.

That year an epidemic of smallpox broke out in the Alta California missions. The terror of the plague spread to San Diego. James

Pattie had some vaccine which his father had kept at the Santa Rita mines; he understood its use. So he got a year on parole to vaccinate the Indians.

He bade his fellow-prisoners good-by. What eventually became of them was never known. He traveled back and forth along the old El Camino Real from San Diego to Sonoma. And finally, in Monterey, he got his freedom. Through the assistance of some American residents, he made his way to Mexico City, seeking redress for what he had suffered.

There is no need to make this story longer in telling the details of that fruitless quest. There came a day when James Ohio Pattie departed from Mexico, broken in spirit, penniless. Kind men helped him on his way. Some months later he came to the Kentucky farm where his grandfather still lived. The other children had married off and scattered to far places. He found himself with no familiar faces about him, save that of the old man whom he had last seen when he was a little child.

It was the same old story—the story of nine great adventures out of ten: hardship and toil and'not a cent to show for it. But the trail which he and his companions had made from Santa Fé down the Gila became one of the great highways by which the restless pioneers reached the Pacific. To-day the railroad train and automobile still follow it. Overhead the aëroplane keeps to its course.

BRIGHAM YOUNG

THE ice and snow were turning gray with the approach of spring. The frozen Mississippi was a leaden expanse between two remote black strips of leafless timber. A line of covered wagons was crossing from the Illinois side. The caravan looked like a string of dots creeping over the drab surface toward the sable woods on the Iowa bank. The iron tires made a creaking sound against the frozen road; it rose toward the lowering sky like a lament.

On the driver's seat of the foremost vehicle was a thick-chested man of middle age. The first impression one got from him was heavy strength. There was no fineness in his lines. Throughout, there was a certain homely indomitability. His face was large and fair; the blue eyes were keen. A brown beard ringed his strong jaw; his upper lip was shaven, revealing the coarse, firm mouth. He would have passed for a well-to-do farmer or a British drover. He was, by trade, a carpenter. By destiny he had become the leader of a people.

That was Brigham Young, head of the Latter-Day Saints, whom we call the Mormons. In the wagons behind his rode the vanguard of twelve thousand followers. On this morning of March 1, 1846, he was leading them forth from their homes into the wilderness.

Those were the days when men took their religion literally and hard, and this new sect, which had originated in western New York, held to some doctrines which their neighbors did not like. So they had wandered westward to Missouri, to be driven back to Nauvoo, Illinois. Here a mob had slain their prophet, Joseph Smith. When the hostility about them had threatened to become a bloody war of extermination, this man Brigham Young, who had become their head, had agreed that the Latter-Day Saints would leave Nauvoo with the coming of the first green grass. But their enemies had continued their outrages. So, at this time, before the wild geese had begun their northward flight, the luckless Mormons left their homes, their stores, their mills and

their temple. They left the carpets on the
floors, the pictures on the walls; they took
with them only the bare necessaries of life.
Where their destination lay they did not know.

Brigham Young had told them that the
Lord would show the way. His belief in this
was literal. His sincerity was absolute. But
there was a wisdom in his big face which did
not belong to a mere fanatic. If the Lord
should choose to put His word into the mouths
of rough-speaking trappers or to set forth
His revelations on the maps of United States
army engineers, this Moses of a later day
was not going to overlook the hint.

The spring thaws broke the ice. The
trains of covered wagons continued coming
from Nauvoo to the Mississippi eastern bank.
Clumsy flatboats carried them across the swollen river among the drifting cakes. The gray
rain fell in sheets. The work of crossing went
on through the long nights. On the Iowa side
the lowlands had become a quagmire. Here,
on small islands at the forest's edge, with the
water lapping all around them and the rain
drumming its dull tune, the women gathered
about huge fires to dry their sodden garments,
while the men were hooking up the teams,

two and three spans to a wagon, to pull out through the viscid mud before the rising river cut them off.

For the most part they were of farmer stock, with a sprinkling of mechanics and small tradesmen. The faith in their leader was born of their religion and tightened by outside opposition; but it was his leadership that kept this faith alive. In these early weeks of their exodus he preached with homely, sometimes vulgar, eloquence. Those sermons held a little of religion and a great deal of instruction as to their daily life. To those who did not hear his voice he took good care that the twelve apostles and the bishops of the wards transmitted the same admonitions. So as they traveled on in those raw spring days, through southern Iowa, the Mormons kept their stock in good order; they husbanded their resources; they hired out along the way to farmers when they got the chance. The covered wagons were their homes; under those canvas tops new babies came into this world and weary souls departed from it. Every morning, before the day's journey was begun, there was an interval of prayer and at its close the company sang a hymn. Always the fa-

vorite was "Zion, Lovely Zion." And even
Brigham did not know where Zion lay.

The rains passed; the days grew warmer.
When May was more than half gone the foremost companies halted about one hundred and
seventy miles west of Nauvoo. Here word
came to them that Elder John C. Little, who
was the agent of their church in Washington,
had offered five hundred men for the Mexican War and that the offer had been accepted
by the President. During the next three weeks
the quota was filled by volunteers and the
battalion marched away to Santa Fé. The
others went on to Council Bluffs and in July
they crossed the Missouri. On a wooded plateau beside the river, six miles north from
where Omaha now stands, Brigham Young
bade them settle down for the time being.
They built sod houses and log cabins. They
erected a long low shed of poles and boughs
for worship and amusement. They called the
place Winter Quarters, and they bided here
until the coming of spring.

During these months Brigham Young made
his plans. Across the summit of the Rockies
lay a wilderness which was known as the
Great American Desert: the land of the mi-

rage, where the few living shrubs were as dry
as ashes. In its center was the Great Salt Lake.
Beside that lake was Zion. In this belief he
ordered the organization of fourteen companies; ten men in every one; and for every
one a captain. He ordered the selection of the
best horses and oxen; the preparation of covered wagons. On the seventh of April, 1847,
he led this advance guard forth to seek the
Promised Land. One thousand miles of trail;
ranges of lofty mountains to be crossed; and
at the end a desert. The children of Israel
only traveled one sixth of the distance, over a
route far easier and in a climate far more
kindly. On this road lurked such savages as
the followers of Moses never dreamed of.

But Brigham Young felt no forebodings.
In the beginning he established a rigid discipline. He maintained it through a tight organization of apostles, counselors and bishops. By theory the company chose its own
leaders. In practice Brigham's word was law.
Every morning at five a bugle roused the
camp. The brethren rose and prayed, attended their teams, got breakfast, and at seven
o'clock they started out. All save the drivers
walked beside the teams, with their rifles in

their hands. A day's journey averaged about twenty miles; and usually there was a two hours' halt at noon. At the end of the march, when there were signs of Indians, the wagons were drawn up in an oval, with the horses and oxen secured inside. At eight-thirty in the evening the bugle sounded and all save the night guard returned to their wagons to pray. At nine o'clock the fires were put out.

The route was by the north bank of the Platte. Here the table-lands were higher and the feed was better than on the southern side, where the regular trail ran. One of the brethren had made a crude instrument somewhat like a modern speedometer, by which a wagon wheel registered the distance traveled. Every few days a record was left—sometimes on a signboard, sometimes on a paper placed in a stone monument, and sometimes it was scrawled on a buffalo skull—giving the miles from Winter Quarters and the local data concerning feed and water.

On Sundays the caravan rested. Toward noontime the members assembled for worship. Now and again, on these Sunday mornings, Brigham Young preached. Here is an excerpt from one of those sermons delivered near Scott's Bluffs:

I have let the brethren dance and fiddle and act the nigger night after night, to see what they would do and what extremes they would go to—but I don't love to see it. The brethren say they want a little exercise to pass the time of evenings, but if you can't tire yourselves enough with a day's journey, why, carry your guns on your shoulders and walk, and carry your wood to camp instead of lounging in your wagons, increasing the loads. Help your teams over mud-holes and bad places—that will give you enough exercise without dancing.

If any man has sense enough to play a game of cards or dance a little without wanting to keep it up all the time, it would be well enough. But you want to keep it up till midnight and all the time. You don't know how to control yourselves. Suppose the angels were witnessing the hoedown the other evening and listening to the haw-haws, would they not be ashamed of it?

I want the brethren to be ready for meeting tomorrow at the appointed time instead of rambling off and hiding in their wagons and playing cards. I think it will be good for us to have a fast-meeting—and a prayer-meeting, and humble ourselves and turn to the Lord.

In such wise—it seems conceivable—Moses
may have dressed down the children of Israel
on occasion.

Early in June, when most of the Oregon-
bound emigrants were leaving Independence
back in Missouri, this little company was at
Fort Laramie, more than five hundred miles
along their road. At the next crossing of the
Platte they made a ferry of logs. The men of
an emigrant train in camp near-by were glad
to pay a dollar and a half a wagon for being
carried across the river. This gave Brigham
Young an idea. He left Thomas Grover and
seven others with the home-made boat, to do
a ferry business with the Gentile caravans
that followed that summer, and to cross the
second expedition of his people, which he
hoped to bring over the plains before autumn.

They went through South Pass. They went
on through the desolate Bitter Creek country.
Jim Bridger, who had discovered the Great
Salt Lake twenty-odd years before, met them
at his trading-post in what is now southwestern
Wyoming and advised with their leaders.
There was, he said, good timber in some of the
valleys leading down to the Great Salt Lake,
but in the basin itself there was no growth save

sage-brush. It was a land of desolation. He offered to give a thousand dollars for an ear of corn raised in that section.

But Brigham Young hung to his idea of the Great Salt Lake. So they left the Oregon Trail and went on across the rugged untracked wilderness north of the Uintah Mountains. They reached the Wasatch range. Now mountain fever was upon them and Brigham Young was a very sick man. But there was seed in these wagons, and the summer was half over. He sent a score of outfits on ahead with the strongest of the men; the others followed. So they made their way across the terrific Wasatch range by Echo and Emigration canyons. On the twenty-third of July the advance guard came out on the table-land overlooking the Salt Lake Valley—a level sage-dotted desert surrounded by lofty mountains. They hurried on down to the flat. When they reached the lowlands—in what is now the northern end of Salt Lake City's business section—they unhooked their teams from the wagons to hitch them up to plows.

The first furrow which they tried showed them the reason for Jim Bridger's gloomy prophecy. The arid soil was as hard as flint.

The steel plowshare broke trying to rend it. Somewhere along that weary road from Nauvoo, Illinois, Brigham Young had learned the Spanish trick of irrigation. Possibly it was from Mormon soldiers returning from Santa Fé. There were those in the advance guard who had heard him speak of it. Nearby a creek came down out of the mountains. They set to work and built a dam; they led the water to the flat. So they moistened the earth and softened it. The next day the main body came down here and found a patch of land already plowed; planted with potatoes.

Brigham Young was still weak from his illness on that twenty-fourth day of July in 1847. But his weakness did not prevent his taking hold of affairs. He called his right-hand man, Heber Kimball, and the others of the twelve apostles into conference, and before sunset this group of sunburned and bearded high priests were listening to his plans for a great city, for rows of green trees and for lush fields to rise from the long arid flats where the gray clumps of sage cast sharp black shadows on the hot sands. The next day was Sunday and he was unable to stand long enough to preach. So Heber Kimball delivered the sermon.

"I want you to put all the seed into the ground that you think will come to maturity. Strive to work righteousness in the beginning, inasmuch as we have reached the Promised Land. I want every man to be as industrious as possible—and get into the ground all the turnips, cabbages and other seeds you can."

On Monday Brigham Young was on his feet and leading an exploring party over the surrounding hills. Before the week was half-way over, the site of Salt Lake City was surveyed and platted; he was arranging the details for a migration of fifteen hundred souls from Winter Quarters this same summer.

Within the month the party built a fort, partly of logs which they hauled seven miles from the mountains, partly of adobe bricks. It inclosed ten acres of ground and within it were two acres of low buildings. Outside the walls they planted ten acres of garden vegetables and forty acres of grain.

On the twenty-second day of August, Brigham Young preached a good-by sermon to those whom he left here to hold down the camp.

"I wish this people may grow and increase and become a great nation. Don't be so devilish hoggish as to be afraid to do a day's work without getting pay for it. I can prophesy in the name of Jesus Christ a man having such a spirit will be damned. Get up your walls four and a half feet high and that will keep the cattle out. In the spring remove your fence. Plow a trench about twenty feet from the houses and the women can raise a multitude of garden sauce." These passages are typical of the discourse.

On the next day he started back across the plains with one hundred men to Winter Quarters. During the latter part of September they brought more than fifteen hundred men, women and children, with three thousand head of stock, across the long trail to Zion.

Fresh snow began to show along the summits of the Wasatch Mountains. The winter came on. For many of these new arrivals there were no cabins. Some of them built dugouts in the hillside; a larger number took the beds of their covered wagons and laid them upon the ground. These were their homes until the spring. That covered-wagon habit has endured among the Mormon people until this day.

With the first warm weather they made new dams in the canyon mouths. They dug long ditches on the hillsides, leading down the water to the plain. They erected the first buildings along the streets which they had laid out the summer before. To every door a rivulet of mountain water flowed. And as the city grew through after-years, the clear streams continued to run beside its streets. You will find them there to-day.

During that summer of 1848, when the crops were nearing maturity, a swarm of beetles crept up across the sage-brush plain; they covered the fields; the green growth began to melt away before them. The last speck of grain seemed doomed. Then, while the elders were offering up prayers, there came from the Salt Lake a myriad of sea-gulls. They fed upon the insects, and one third of the crop was saved. In memory of that occasion there is a statue of a sea-gull in the temple grounds.

New wagon trains came on across the plains. Four thousand people were in Zion now. In the next winter food ran short. Three quarters of a pound of flour daily to the person was the ration. Many a family went out into the hills to dig the bulbs of the sego lily from beneath the snow. So this plant which helped to save them from starvation was chosen fifty years later by their children and their children's children as the state flower of Utah.

In that year of 1848 Brigham Young sent an expedition by the route which the Salt Lake, San Pedro & Los Angeles branch of the Union Pacific system now travels. These wagons crossed southwestern Utah and Nevada; they went on over the flaming Armagosa and Mojave deserts to Cajon Pass on the cost range of southern California. Here they founded the town of San Bernardino.

In 1849 the great gold rush came, to find in the midst of the savage intermountain wilderness a city surrounded by green fields and seedling orchards; to find new trails beyond already beaten down to wagon roads.

Then, in the early fifties, when the pioneers were settling down in comfort, when the civilization which they had established was reaching out into remote valleys of Utah, the Mormon migration from the East came to its climax in one of the bravest episodes of the Overland Trail.

There were in England some thousands of

new converts to the Mormon faith. A large proportion of them were too poor to make the journey to Salt Lake by wagon outfits. So Brigham Young helped the heads of the British missions to evolve a plan for these people to travel across the wilderness afoot. With the aid of a few wagons, they were to haul their possessions in two-wheeled carts.

In the summer of 1856 more than fifteen hundred of these English emigrants started from Iowa City, the terminus of the railroad. They went in five companies. Some were of peasant stock, some were laborers and small artisans from English towns. The ways of the wilderness were a sealed book to them. Only their captains knew the road.

The last three of these companies were delayed by lack of carts. July was near its end before the final outfit began to cross the State of Iowa. They reached old Winter Quarters, six miles north of Omaha, late in August.

Their carts were much like those which paper-hangers used to push, with wheels set for the width of the wagon track. The weight of one was sixty pounds. The load was two hundred pounds. The owner stood between the shafts, breasting the cross-bar, and dragged the clumsy little vehicle along the rutted trail.

So they started up the Platte, with a trio of laden wagons bringing up the rear of each company and a few cattle being driven on ahead. Men and women trudged along the dusty trail, some of the mothers with babes at their breasts. In the mornings they gathered for prayer; their hymns rang out. Rough going now; deep dust and sand; steep pitches where they crossed the gullies. The young and strong strode on between the shafts; the old men and women and the children lagged.

Now they were averaging fifteen miles a day. About the fires of evenings they laughed and they sang. "O Zion, Lovely Zion" was the favorite hymn. The days went by. Some of the carts were wearing out. They mended tires with tin cans, with plates and kettles from their mess outfits. The shrieking of the dry axles could be heard for miles.

The feed began to get sparser. Passing herds of buffalo stampeded the work oxen and horses. They yoked up young stock and milch cows; but these were unable to move the wagons, and every hand-cart took on another sack of flour. The progress slackened; the women helped their husbands in the shafts;

the weary little children begged for rides. There was no longer laughter by the fires at night.

A party of returning missionaries passed them, going west, and exhorted them to be of good cheer. But as they went on, the missionaries shook their heads. It looked like an early winter. They hurried their teams in the hope of reaching Salt Lake in time to get relief back to these people.

On the second of September the fourth company reached Fort Laramie, and James G. Willie, their captain, called a meeting of the men to look over their situation. A recapitulation showed that if they kept on at their present rate their flour would be exhausted before they were within three hundred miles of Salt Lake. The daily allowance was reduced to a pound. They tried to travel faster. The road grew rougher and their pace was slower. At Independence Rock the ration was cut to twelve ounces for a workingman; nine ounces for a woman or an old man; four to eight ounces for a child.

A sage-brush upland and the wind came sweeping bitter cold from the mountains at night. Their blankets and clothing were barely enough for summer weather. Alkali water was bringing on dysentery. Scanty food was aggravating the sickness. They waded ice-cold streams. The women kilted up their skirts, helping the men drag the rickety carts through the swift current. Only a few of the children walked now. Some of them were barely able to cling to the lurching loads. The old began to droop and die.

On the Sweetwater there were many crossings. Ice clung to the banks. Sick and weary women strove to comfort their gaunt babies when they cried for food. Young fellows who had been lusty at Winter Quarters were staggering between the shafts. In the evening, when they pitched camp, the able-bodied carried the sick from the wagons, to warm themselves beside the fires. Now, in the mornings, they began to find the dead lying in their blankets frozen stiff.

The snow came and the wind howled across the harsh uplands. The cattle strayed away by night before the storms. They buried their dead every morning, five and six in one grave, wrapped in their blankets. Then they prayed and sang and started on.

The flour was gone. They killed the few

emaciated cattle which were left. The sickness was increasing. Men sank down and died between the shafts of the hand-carts. The first blizzard of an early winter swooped down upon them as they toiled up the long grades toward South Pass.

In the month of October the Mormons were holding the annual conference in Salt Lake City. The first three hand-cart companies had already arrived in fairly good shape. Now there came the party of missionaries who had passed the others. One of these missionaries was Joseph A. Young, a son of Brigham's. His father sent him back along the road the next morning, and behind him two wagon outfits bearing food and blankets.

The fourth company were near South Pass when Joseph Young met them. Some of those whom he came upon were lying dead beside the trail. The living were so weak that it took six of them to get a single hand-cart up a hill. He left them and hurried on to tell his news of the relief trains to Edward Martin's company one hundred miles behind them. On the morning after he went, there were thirteen dead to bury in a single grave. The survivors rested that day in camp, and two more died beside the fires. They started on the next morning; and they met the first relief train west of South Pass. Out of four hundred and twenty who had left Winter Quarters, sixty-seven had died along the way. In the Martin company of more than five hundred the dead numbered above one hundred and fifty.

It was late in November when the wagons brought the last survivors down over the benchlands which overlook the valley of the Great Salt Lake.

Ten years had passed since that exodus from Nauvoo began. Salt Lake City was a young metropolis; a dozen towns were thriving in the basin along the western edge of the Wasatch Mountains. Back of this accomplishment there were three elements. Perhaps you will see two of them more plainly by brief incidents.

An old man whose white beard covered half his chest told the writer one of them, some twenty years ago, in a little Utah village. He drove a wagon in the expedition sent out from Salt Lake City for relief of the hand-cart companies. On the seat beside him was a bishop, a man of rough speech and rougher ways, who was believed to be gifted with the power of the laying on of hands.

It was evening when their wagon reached the lonely sage-brush upland where the company was camped. A bitter wind was blowing and fires blazed beside the trail. In the light of one of these fires they saw a woman on her knees, with three little children huddling around her, and on the frozen earth the rigid form of a man outstretched. She turned her face toward them, worn with hardship, ravaged with a sorrow so deep that even the sight of these wagons bringing food did nothing to allay it.

Her husband, she told them, had just died.

Then the bishop climbed down from his seat and he knelt beside her. He prayed for power. He laid his hands upon the still form. And life came back. The next morning the man was riding in one of the wagons.

As to what did take place there on that evening in the snow the writer does not even pretend to speculation. But the old man who told that story believed what he was telling. And this literal deep faith, which was so widespread among those people—a faith which made them take the word of Brigham

Young as inspired—was the main reason for the things which he accomplished.

The other incident took place a year or two ago. A number of us were riding in a closed car on the Salt Lake-Ogden highway, when the driver's wife asked him to stop at a stand where fruit was being sold. She knew the place of old, she said; and they had plums of unusual flavor. Pottawatomie plums, they were called. The name carried suggestion, which for some time remained unanswered. Until I happened to remember that the trail by which many of the Mormons traveled to the Platte ran for some seventy-odd miles up the Pottawatomie River in southeastern Nebraska. The seeds from which these Utah fruit trees originated had been carried across the plains by some thrifty emigrant.

It was by this spirit that these people made two blades of grass grow where even the traditional one had not grown before.

The third element behind the migration was Brigham Young. His was the mind that nursed the faith and thrift which sustained them in the transplanting of a people. He was in many ways a crude man. There was in him something of the brutality which belongs to those close to the earth. There are chapters in his story which are not pleasant to read. But he was a man of faith and his works were mighty.

JOHN AUGUSTUS SUTTER

WHATEVER you choose to call it—
Fate, Destiny, or Divine Providence
—that power is the real hero of this story. As
for Sutter, he was an instrument; all his work
and exploits were, without his knowing it, de-
signed to further a nation's fortunes. If you
look at it in any other way than this, the narrative is bound to be bitterly ironical, for the
force which directs this world's events has no
time to waste in working out the happiness
of individuals.

From the beginning the gold was there,
nuggets and flakes and fine dust, gleaming in
the gravel of the California foothills. And
the Spaniards who came to this El Dorado
were the greatest gold-seekers on the Western
Hemisphere. It was from a fable of an island,
rich in the precious metal, that they named the
land. But when they settled along its seaward
valleys, these people, whose forefathers had
marched long marches and fought bloody battles and laid proud cities waste for the yellow

stuff, stayed almost within sound of the surf; they rarely ventured east of the coast range.

While the Spanish settlements drowsed about their missions in the valleys by the sea, this man Sutter went bankrupt in a little Swiss town at the edge of the Black Forest and started on the long trek to rehabilitate his fortunes. Then the descendants of the old conquistadores were doomed to see an alien people invading their back country. They were doomed to see the wealth which they had missed—the riches of which their avid forefathers had fondly dreamed—taken away by strangers. And this is only the beginning of those ends which John A. Sutter unwittingly brought about.

It was in Santa Fé, New Mexico, that he first got the idea of going to California. Three years of fortune-seeking had kept him moving toward the setting sun, working at many jobs, dealing with many kinds of men; he was now a full-fledged hyphenated American, one of that breed who drank their beer or light wine very slowly, spoke with a thick accent, and were to be found not only in the seaboard cities but in every nook of the western wilderness which the pioneers had penetrated.

John A. Sutter

Johann August Suter was the way he had written his name back in Basel; now he called himself John A. Sutter; a rawboned man of thirty-five and single-purposed to the point of obstinacy.

In that summer of 1837 the sandy plaza in the center of the old City of the Holy Faith was always resounding with the *crack-crack* of the long bull whips, the braying of mules, the twanging drawl of Missouri teamsters, the softer voices of the Mexicans who came in crowds to buy calicoes and hardware and knickknacks. Weather-stained men who had made the long journey across the prairies and the Rocky Mountains from St. Joseph dickered with plump señoras who looked like magnified black beetles; with swarthy señores wearing plush trousers slashed below the knee, and huge sombreros; with señoritas whose eyes were like sable velvet. Among the tobacco-chewing merchants was Sutter—but he was not of them. For his dreams were flavored with European longings—longings for land and crops and an army of husbandmen. Gold to him was but a means to forward that end.

In this old city whose narrow streets wound

away from the plaza's four sides, among the flat-roofed adobe buildings, he met an adventurer whose long journey was from the west.

One of these Americans—trappers and traders who had struck out a year or two before from Santa Fé with saddle horses and pack trains to take the weary trail across southwestern deserts and arid mountain ranges to the pueblo of Los Angeles—had returned to tell of the missions in the fertile valleys, of cattle herds and vineyards and grain fields. He found this Swiss an eager listener. And when Sutter went back to St. Joseph, Missouri, with his covered wagons and his profits from the summer's trading, he carried an idea. It grew during the long days of the journey, and during the next winter it fastened tightly on him. He managed to find an American Fur Company trader of the name of Dripps, who was setting out by way of the North Platte trail to the annual rendezvous in the Wind River country, in April, 1838.

That year the migration to Oregon by way of the South Pass was pretty well begun. So Sutter wasted little time with the blanketed Indians and the bearded trappers in buckskin

who brought their beaver skins to the rendezvous in the quaking asp grove among the
mountains somewhere west of where Fort
Washakie stands to-day. He joined one of the
outfits that were passing through to the south
of there, and made his way by the old Snake
River to Oregon.

Getting to California in those days was no
simple matter. He spent some time with the
Hudson's Bay people at Fort Vancouver—
long enough to satisfy himself that an overland journey southward would land him at
his destination very probably in no shape to
establish the little empire of which he
dreamed. So he got passage in a vessel for the
Sandwich Islands. It was a good year before
he reached the somnolent village of Yerba
Buena—which was to become the roaring city
of San Francisco. He came by way of Sitka,
Alaska—a long roundabout trail from St.
Joseph, Missouri, but in all its length he stuck
to the idea of California and the little empire
which he was going to establish. The brig
which had brought him was badly battered
by storms; and the authorities gave Sutter
barely time for necessary repairs before sending him to Monterey, the port of entry. Here,

at the head of the winding street which still
leads inland from the tile-roofed old custom-
house, he called on Governor Alvarado in his
adobe mansion and told him of his plans: to
take the eight Kanakas and the six white mechanics whom he had brought with him from
the Sandwich Islands, into the interior of
California; preferably to the Sacramento
Valley; to establish a settlement; to till the
lands; to run his cattle in the hills; to grind
meal, make wine, tan leather and engage in
trades. That was Sutter's proposition. And
Governor Alvarado had good reasons for
harkening to such plans; for in those days
the valleys of the San Joaquin and the Sacramento were infested by outlaw bands. Indians
who had escaped from the missions and joined
the inland tribes led their companions in constant forays on the settlements. At Mission
San José and throughout the Santa Clara Valley the ranchos suffered constant depreda-
tions. The Mexican soldiery at the presidios
along the coast were helpless when it came to
expeditions of reprisal. Here now was one
who promised, if his project worked out, to
be in command of an outpost: a man of parts
and of means who might go far in subduing

these swarthy horse thieves. His frontier post would always be a buffer to receive the brunt of their wild attacks. So Governor Alvarado told Sutter to go by all means to the valley of the Sacramento River and establish himself there; to come back in a year for citizenship papers and a title to what lands he might select.

Late in the summer of 1839 Sutter, his eight Kanakas and five white men left Yerba Buena on a schooner, with several small boats. It took them eight days, searching through the tule marshes where the Sacramento and the San Joaquin form their delta, to find the former river's mouth. They sailed up-stream, between the reed-fringed flatlands. Great clouds of wild fowl rose before them; they came among the wide oak-dotted plains where the grass grew almost waist high. Near where Sacramento stands to-day they were confronted by two hundred Indians in war paint; but, to the Swiss-American who had seen the Pawnees, the Comanches and the bloodthirsty Sioux, these natives were not so formidable as they were to the Spanish officers. He landed, made his peace with them, and went on up-stream one hundred miles or so.

Then his hands began to show symptoms of mutiny and he turned back. Of the country which he had seen, the section around the present site of Sacramento seemed most promising. He landed his cargo of foodstuffs and agricultural tools at the mouth of the American River. Three of the white mechanics went back to Yerba Buena. With the other two and the Kanakas he pitched his first camp in the live-oak groves not very far from the spot where California's Capitol building stands to-day. With a regard for the traditions of their commonwealth which other western people would do well to emulate, the latter-day populace have restored the walled inclosure and the buildings into which this first camp grew, and you may see them now just as they were when Sutter's Fort was the stronghold of early American occupation.

During that winter of 1839–40 the renegade Indians from the coast valleys saw their sanctuary threatened by this first invasion of the white man and determined to get rid of him. They led small war parties down from the foothills to massacre the little group in the tents and reed-roofed huts among the live-oaks. Of Sutter's retainers the most trust-

worthy was a big white dog, part bull terrier
and part mastiff. Thrice when the savages
were creeping on their bellies through the
darkness, the animal discovered them and not
only aroused the camp but did his own share
in putting the attacking party to flight.

So the savages saw the cluster of tents grow
to a group of adobe houses and the original
party increase, through American wanderers
who came from Yerba Buena, and vaqueros
who were hired from coastwise ranchos, to
about twenty men. By the spring of 1840
something like a thousand cattle, purchased
from the Sunol and Martinez ranchos down
near salt water, were grazing on the green
flats; the Kanakas were cutting a road through
the thick live-oak groves to the Sacramento
River's bank, where several white men were
building a boat-landing—an *embarcadero,* the
Californians called it. Young grain was beginning to film a large plowed field with
emerald. Then the renegades knew the good
old days were over unless they wiped out this
crowd of interlopers at once.

There were formidable men among these
outlaws: some of them full-blooded Indians,
some of them mongrels with a streak of the

presidio Spanish. They sought out the Cosumnes Indians, one of the most warlike of the
foothill tribes, and held council with them in
a red flanked gulch where the Sierras come
down to the valley plains. When the dancing
and the pipe-smoking were over, about three
hundred Cosumnes daubed their bodies with
war-paint and set forth for Sutter's camp.

But while all these preparations were being made a friendly native stole away and
brought the news to Sutter. The latter left a
number of well-armed men in the little settlement and took eight reliable hands away with
him. They set out by night on good horses and
rode hard to the first foothills. Here they
made camp at dawn and waited for the next
night. When darkness came they went on
through the rolling country where the jack-
oaks and the long-plumed digger pines mingle, until they came to the canyon where the
war party were in camp. Daybreak found the
eight of them lying behind the crest of a
ridge; and when the savages began to stir
down in the poppy and lupin-spangled ravine
bed below them, they opened fire. The fight
that followed was brief; it was a case of bows
and arrows against long-barreled rifles: just

JOHN AUGUSTUS SUTTER 189

a massacre and a disordered rout. When the powder smoke drifted away, Sutter's men counted twenty dead savages sprawled on the gold and purple flower carpet.

So, by the old trick of the red men which he had learned from their fiercer brethren back in the sage-brush country, Sutter awed this tribe; and before the grass began to turn yellow with the summer's heat, their chiefs came down from the hills to smoke the pipe of peace with him. From that time on their young men brought furs to barter for his beads and traders' gewgaws; they hired out to him as laborers; they fought for him against the other savages.

That summer Sutter went down to drowsy Monterey and got his citizenship papers, together with his land grant—forty-eight thousand acres. He was appointed representative of the governor, with power to administer justice on this northern frontier of California.

During these years of the early forties a few Americans were dribbling into the territory; some from coastwise vessels and some down the long rough trail from Oregon. Of the wanderers, a good share found their way to Sutter's growing settlement. He welcomed them and gave them work. The grain-fields were spreading wider; the herds of cattle and horses were increasing; more adobe buildings went up.

Now the Russians, who held a portion of northern California near the mouth of the river which still bears their name, were preparing to leave the country. One day, late in the summer of 1841, their governor, Alexander Rotchoff, arrived at Sutter's landing on the schooner *Sacramento,* and offered all the colony's property to the Swiss for thirty thousand dollars. Sutter went back with him to Fort Ross, looked over the holdings and accepted the proposition. That autumn his men drove two thousand head of cattle, together with as many sheep and horses, from the coast to the Sacramento Valley; they brought a large quantity of tools and foodstuffs by water, and with them fifteen cannon. John Sutter built a wall eighteen feet high inclosing a space five hundred by one hundred feet about his adobe buildings. He mounted the ordnance upon it. The erection of that wall— the planting of those cannon—marked a turning point in California history.

At this time, when the strained relations

preliminary to the Mexican War were making Americans unwelcome here—just when these same Americans were beginning to appear in larger and larger numbers—Sutter's Fort was the one stronghold in all the territory worthy of its name. For that reason it became the haven for the vanguard of explorers and settlers from the United States.

Commodore Wilkes, who had been sent out by Congress to explore the west coast, came down overland from Oregon with a handful of trail-worn marines and officers to rest here and replenish his supplies.

Captain John C. Frémont and Kit Carson journeyed from Oregon across the Siskiyous with a handful of half-starved followers and three or four gaunted pack-mules. Sutter fed them and furnished them fresh outfits which enabled them to travel back overland to the Rockies.

Meantime, east of the Mississippi men were loading their covered wagons with food and farm implements, leaving their homes for the long trail to Oregon. The lure of free land— and the lure of adventure—were sweeping the young nation like an epidemic. The overland migration was on; the route which the trappers had discovered less than twenty years before across the continent's backbone was becoming a well-beaten road.

Now many of these restless farmers were beginning to hear talk of a more alluring land than Oregon. Richard Henry Dana's "Two Years Before the Mast" was being widely read; the weekly papers were printing everything they could get hold of concerning the kindly country Dana described. Bearded trappers were telling Missouri villagers of the drowsy, sun-warmed valleys west of the Sierras, where chills and fever were unknown. And in the year 1841 the wheel tracks which had hitherto led on, without a break, across the sage-brush plains of the Snake River Valley were split at Fort Hall. The new fork led off to the southwest; it marked the course of a wagon train led by John Bidwell, across an untracked wilderness. Twenty-five men and one woman, they drove their gaunted oxen over the glaring alkali flats west of the Great Salt Lake; on through the scorched reaches of the Carson Sink, where to this day the mirage unfolds its wavering curtains before the eyes of speeding motorists; on up the eastern slopes of the Sierras to the Sonora

Pass. Their wagons had been abandoned; the oxen carried the remnants of the supplies on their backs. The party wandered down the long ridges between the north and middle forks of the Stanislaus River. And one day late in the autumn they came, half-starved, to Sutter's Fort. Here Bidwell and some others of them found employment; and when the rest had recruited their strength they scattered through the lower Sacramento Valley.

That was the beginning. Three years later the Stevens Murphy wagon train left the first wheel tracks across the Sierras by the pass where the Central Pacific trains now thunder through the snowsheds. The year after that more than two hundred and fifty emigrants straggled down through the red foothills to Sutter's walled inclosure beside the Sacramento River. Now new ranches began to appear hereabouts, and Sutter's Fort became a trading-place, the center of the American population. Men came hither for food, for seed, for tools—and oftentimes for help.

One February day in 1847, at Johnson's ranch near where the town of Wheatland stands to-day, seven horrible forms appeared in the gray winter rain—five women and two men. They looked more like skeletons, made by some grotesque trick to shamble forward on their feet, than like living beings. Their emaciated faces bore the black scars of old frost-bites; and in their eyes was the horror of memories that would not die. To those at the ranch they told such of their story as they could bear to repeat.

The Forlorn Hope—so they had called themselves thirty-two days before. There had been nine men and six women in that party then. They had left seventy others, snowbound and starving, at a lake near the summit of the Truckee Pass, choosing rather to risk death in this terrible journey on foot through the deep drifts than to face its certainty by staying with those companions.

Now a messenger carried the news from Johnson's ranch to Sutter's Fort. And from Sutter's Fort one relief expedition after another went up into the Sierras to rescue the survivors by that lake. They made their way through forty-foot drifts; they carried food and blankets on their backs. This and subsequent expeditions brought the survivors of the death-camp down into the valley.

So forty-five of the seventy-nine who had

made up the ill-fated Donner party came through the horrors of that winter. Ill luck and poor leadership had combined against these Illinois farmers all the way across the plains and mountains; and early snows had entrapped them as they were struggling to the summit of the Sierras. It was due to John Sutter's men and food that any of them lived.

Sutter's men and Sutter's food; Sutter's walls and Sutter's cannon. By them the gate to California was held open to Americans. The wagon trains kept coming in. The settlers spread through the Sacramento and the Sonoma valleys. When the Mokolumne Indians wakened to the dangers of the invasion, and started to wipe out the new-comers, Sutter led thirty men up the Calaveras River against them. In an all-day battle his party killed more than their own number of savages and the Indian menace became a thing of the past.

During the late forties the three-acre inclosure on the oak-dotted flatlands was a busy place. Within the high adobe wall there were: a blacksmith shop, where men were shoeing horses, making plows and mending tools; a huge wine-press; a grist-mill, whose stones had been brought down from the higher foot-hills. Carpenters and wheelwrights were busy making wagons. Indian women were forever at work, carding wool and weaving blankets. In the morning the vaqueros rode forth to make the long day's round of the distant herds. Laborers left to till the fields of grain. Boat-men came up from the river landing; and not a week passed but one or two cargoes ar-rived at the *embarcadero* from the bay of San Francisco. The Indians brought down their furs from the foothills to trade for beads and gewgaws. In the midst of all these activities Sutter lived like an old feudal lord. Now and again some visitor of note came up from the distant bay and got royal entertainment. The little empire had grown from a dream to reality. Its owner called it New Helvetia, and now he sent to Europe for his wife and family.

The Bear Flag rebellion had passed, find-ing him loyal to the Mexican Government. The Mexican War was over. Sutter looked into the future—

"Next year more than one thousand emi-grants will come," he told his clerk, John Bidwell.

It was January, 1848, when he made that

prophecy; long days of rain, when the wide
flatlands melted away into the moist drab
sky-line; brief intervals of sunshine when the
whole valley shone emerald green. John A.
Sutter strode wide-footedly about his fort,
from office to blacksmith shop, from shop to
store, swinging his heavy cane—in his middle
age, ruddy of face, set in his ways, sure with
prosperity. A multitude of projects were in
his mind, some in their inception, some nearing completion—passenger boats plying between his *embarcadero* and Yerba Buena;
more thousands of acres in grain; fruit trees
from old Fort Ross to be transplanted for
new orchards; a distillery for brandies and
high wines; new muskets for his soldiers. He
was the lord of a principality as large as the
Grand Duchy of Baden, where he had grown
up as a boy. He saw larger domains ahead of
him.

His thoughts went to his most recent project, conceived to meet the next year's growing demands—a sawmill, some forty miles
away as the crow flies, on the South Fork of
the American River. It was just about built
now. Almost any day he looked for the man
in charge to come with news of the first log

on the skids. He pictured the yellow lumber floating down-stream, to make more buildings, to be sold to Sam Brannan, the Mormon storekeeper, and others who were establishing themselves outside the fort. And while his mind was busy with that picture, the Fate which had held the gold-hungry Spanish to the coastward valleys during all these decades was working out its ends at this same saw-mill.

John W. Marshall was in charge of that work; he was in partnership with Sutter in the enterprise. A carpenter by trade, he had been a farmer in the Ohio Valley, a settler on the prairies near Fort Leavenworth, a trapper in the Rockies. Then he had wandered on to Oregon and thence had come southward to New Helvetia, to become one of Sutter's most trusted henchmen. Just now he was having a little trouble with the tail-race of the mill.

A dozen white men and as many Indians were cutting logs. The little building where the timber was to be rendered into lumber was complete, upon a benchland beside the South Fork of the American River. If you are curious as to the spot, look for the town of Coloma on the California map. The race needed deepening before the water-wheel could whirl the saw. So the gate was left open every evening, and during the nights the rushing current scoured out the channel. Every morning Marshall came down from his cabin on the pine-dotted hillside to see what progress had been made.

On the morning of January 24 Marshall went as usual to the mill. An Indian shut off the water and picked out the most of the boulders which the strong current had carried down the race. Marshall stepped into the channel. Near its lower end he saw upon a rock a flake of yellow metal. He picked it up. Its sides were worn smooth. It was irregular along the edges, about the size and shape of a small melon seed. Its weight made him suspicious. He hammered it upon a granite boulder; it was malleable. Now he was fairly sure that it was gold.

He gathered up more flakes, about an ounce of them. He showed his find to some of the men that evening in the bunk-house. It roused mild curiosity among them.

"When I go down to the fort, I'll have the

old man test it out," he said. And during the four days' interval the matter was almost as good as forgotten.

A rainy day the twenty-eighth of January. When John Marshall came to Sutter's Fort the afternoon was drawing on toward evening; a heavy gray downpour hastened the darkness. John Bidwell, the clerk, was working on some accounts in the office where Sutter greeted his partner-employee.

"I've something important to tell you," Marshall said. The two of them retired to an inner room and closed the door. Marshall unwrapped a soiled rag and showed an ounce or two of yellow flakes. Sutter tested some of them with acids; then by specific gravity.

"Twenty-three-carat gold." His voice betrayed excitement. "By Jo, we have got to keep this quiet for a while, or I will lose some of my men before the mill is done."

Two days later Marshall returned to the mill.

"Oh, boys, by God, it is the pure stuff," he told the men. But the excitement still remained mild. Four days afterward he hurried to the bunk-house and announced that Sutter had come out to see what the discovery amounted to. It was a sunny Sunday morning and all hands wanted some fun to pass the time away. So—

"We'll scatter some of the flakes in the tail-race," Marshall proposed. "Then we'll let the old man find them. That will make him so excited, he'll bring out his bottle and give us all a drink."

They followed out his instructions. Soon Sutter came down the hill from Marshall's cabin, swinging his cane, walking wide-footedly. The men waited in silence. But the small son of Peter Wimmer had seen the salted mill-race and he ran up the slope to meet the lord of New Helvetia with a fistful of gold.

"By Jo!" John Sutter cried, "it is rich." And so the men got their drink after all.

News like that could not stay suppressed. On March 15 the "Alta Californian" came out in San Francisco with a two-inch item announcing the find. But the newly chris-tened town down by the bay showed fully as much interest in the preceding item, which told how W. A. Liedesdorff's horse had won yesterday's race at Mission Dolores.

Meantime, one of the mill-hands who had

come down to Sutter's Fort traded some of the
gold dust for a drink of whisky to Sam Brannan, the Mormon elder who kept a trading-
post outside the walls. And shortly afterward
Brannan woke up sleepy little San Francisco
to a realization of what had really happened.

Then the rush began.

In that summer of 1848, while Monterey
and San Francisco and San José and every
pueblo along the California coast were empty-
ing their people into the foothills about the
American River, Fate—had it been blest with
a sense of humor—must have chuckled. For
it was then that Mexico turned California
over to the United States.

Twelve months later the eager thousands
were on their way, by ship and covered wagon,
to the banks of the Sacramento. Thousands
and then more thousands. Their wagon trains
came winding down the long ridges of the
Sierras; the schooners which brought them
up from San Francisco Bay were laden low
with passengers. And one idea was in every
mind—Gold.

John Sutter's employees had long since
joined the rush. No one was left to tend his
fields, to reap his grain, to guard his herds.

The new-comers pastured their horses and oxen on his uncut wheat. They killed his cattle for meat. They built their cabins on the lands which his men had plowed. And all this time the singleness of purpose which had held him to the building of his little empire remained with him. He paid no attention to the stored riches in the hills.

The town of Sacramento grew with mushroom swiftness where his crops had grown. By some freak of unkind laws, the United States refused to recognize his title to these lands. With his wife and family, who had come from Europe to share his prosperity, John Sutter moved away from New Helvetia, a ruined man. By strange coincidence, John Marshall also failed to take advantage of his discovery; and, failing, was made poor by the inrushing gold-seekers who stole his cattle and his lands. In their later years these two men lived on pensions granted to them by the State of California.

And now the placer beds of California gave the United States the gold which kept the nation solvent during the Civil War. They brought the swift migration, which in its turn brought the transcontinental railroads. They created a new breed of pioneer—the American prospector—who penetrated every untrodden corner of the wilderness.

So Alder Gulch and Last Chance brought thousands into western Montana, and the Bozeman Trail was beaten down into a well-traveled road through the hunting grounds of the Sioux and the Cheyenne. Denver lured multitudes, who spread over the eastern slope of the Colorado Rockies. Deadwood came into being and forthwith the Black Hills passed from the Indians. The wanderers with shovels and gold-pans drifted northward into the Caribou, on to Telegraph Creek, on to Forty Mile beside the distant Yukon. Other wanderers, with prospectors' picks instead of shovels, uncovered veins of quartz; the mother lode; the Comstock lode; Leadville's riches; Tombstone's silver. The mountains and the deserts were scarred with beaten roads; the wilderness became a memory.

ALEXANDER MAJORS

IT was in the late fifties when this tall Kentuckian brought his bull teams and huge freight wagons to the Overland Trail. With his coming begins the last chapter in the chronicle of the greatest natural highway in all the world.

To get a better idea of the meaning of that chapter, take a look into the past. This road, by which the American people crossed their country, was made by Nature. After the time of Thomas Jefferson, when our Government resolutely turned its back upon the West, fur traders discovered it. Still later on, while some of our greatest statesmen were eloquently describing the Rocky Mountains as an insurmountable wall, beyond which the people of this country would never pass, the wagon outfits of settlers were cutting ruts in the sagebrush uplands which split the waters of the continent at South Pass. Those ruts were numerous and deep down the Snake River to Oregon; several pack outfits and one wagon train had already turned off to cross the Nevada sinks and the Sierras to California when Captain John C. Frémont followed the aging tracks to the Pacific and was hailed in Congress as a pathfinder. There came the Mormon hegira, and the rush of argonauts to Sutter's Mill; Salt Lake City grew to an inland metropolis; Denver was the center of a huge mining boom. The Overland Trail became a highway half a mile wide in places, lined by the wrecks of wagons and the bones of animals, marked here and there by graves.

If you will take a map of these United States and stretch a string from Washington to San Francisco, you will probably be surprised at seeing how nearly that taut line corresponds to the route of this ungraded highway. The shortest distance between two points—and those points were the centers of the East and the West. In the late fifties, when the Civil War was impending, quick communication with the Pacific coast was beginning to be recognized as a military necessity. But the Government at Washington continued to hold its eyes shut to the shorter route—and tried to get this rapid communication with California by subsidizing a round-

OVERLAND ROUTES
TO THE **PACIFIC** 1853 ➤

Statute Miles

about stage line through Texas and the south-western deserts.

Such were the conditions when Alexander Majors came upon the scene. He was still young—in his thirties then; a giant of a man, deep of voice, deliberate in speech and action; but always bold. He belonged to that type of business adventurer which had so much to do with the settlement of the Far West, the type whose offensive tactics were its only asset. He was utterly without the canny caution and the small-eyed thrift by which so many stay-at-homes nurse their savings into fortunes. He had a certain Jovelike splendor in his dealings with his fellows, which sometimes led him to intrust thousands to those who were unworthy. As to his own word, he deemed it sacred. In one respect he was somewhat unique along the Overland Trail. Like young Jedediah Smith, who was among those trappers discovering the route more than twenty years before, he was a devout Christian.

Down on the old Santa Fé Trail he had been a freighter in his youth. There his bull teams had made the broadhorn record—ninety days for the round trip from Independence

to the City of the Holy Faith. Now his oxen
and Conestoga wagons were hauling goods
up the Platte to Julesburg; up the South
Platte to the roaring camp of Denver; up
the North Platte to Bridger's Fort and Salt
Lake. Six to twelve yoke of oxen to a wagon;
twenty-five four-ton wagons to a train; two
hundred and fifty trains. He had an army of
seven thousand men on his pay-roll.

When any of those wagon trains pulled out
of Independence for the long haul to Denver
or the Great Salt Lake, it had but one certainty ahead of it—the certainty of trouble
somewhere along the road. On the wide grass-
covered prairies the trouble was never more
serious than muddy ground or boggy ford;
but when the outfit passed beyond the green
carpet to the land of the sage-brush and the dog
towns and the buffalo—then its progress was
attended by real hazards and wild action.

For some of the plains Indians were getting
bad during these years of the late fifties. Even
among the tribes which were still at peace,
there were young warriors lusting for the
glory and the wealth to be gained by running
off the white man's horses. And every wagon
train took along a good-sized *caballada*. So

on the wide sage-brush plateaus which climb
imperceptibly toward the snow peaks of the
Continental Divide many a stand was made
in the shelter of a circle of wagons, with the
weather-stained teamsters lying on their bellies under the vehicles, using their muzzle-
loading rifles with slow precision against the
wider circle of naked warriors whooping
round them on their bare-backed ponies.
Indian-fighting was regarded as a part of the
business, and the trip was deemed unusual
which went by without at least a skirmish.
Among the wagon masters some became noted
for their skill as warriors. Of these Lew Simpson was perhaps the most widely known for
his exploits. Simpson took on a thin sixteen-
year-old boy as a roustabout in eastern Kansas
during one of his trips. The youngster's name
was Willie Cody, but before he left the em-
ploy of Alexander Majors the Willie was re-
placed by Bill; he was already becoming
famous along the Overland Trail as pony express rider, stage driver and Indian-fighter.

Aside from its hazards, the freighting business of Alexander Majors had the glamour of
picturesqueness. One of those trains was a
sight long to be remembered: On the high

seat of every wagon a driver, weather-stained, with the dust of the weary trails settled deep into his garments; in his hand the short-stocked bull whip. Ahead of him the long double file of oxen, bowing to their wooden yokes; obedient to his voice—or, when they lagged, responding to the accurately placed forty-foot lash. So the train of twenty-five vehicles toiled on, with the wagon master riding in the lead; the spare cattle and horses driven by a herder in the rear; and over all a dense cloud of dust that climbed into the heavens. On a clear day you could see that signal twenty miles away. When the wind was right and the outfit was meeting heavy pulling, you could hear the *pop-popping* of the bull whips for a good two miles.

At intervals along the trail Alexander Majors had established feed stations, where baled hay and grain were kept in warehouses. Here settlements grew up; and when the trains came in, the sunburned bullwhackers lined up at the unpainted pine bars to cut the alkali dust that had gathered in their throats with the potent whisky of the sagebrush country. Best known of all these stations was old Julesburg, near the forks of the

Alexander Maiors

North and South Platte trails. Over the long intervals between these stopping-places the trains hauled their feed; and at night the men gathered their huge wagons in a circle within which they made their camp.

So the adventurous business went on. Then, while it was at its height, while the threat of the Civil War was growing blacker every month, Alexander Majors enlarged his field of operations by buying out a decrepit little stage line which was making a pretense of carrying mails and passengers between St. Joseph, Missouri, and Denver. In the new venture there came to him two partners. And the firm was known as Russell, Majors & Waddell. Of its members, the last named was an accountant, and his activities were largely confined to the books; the first was an enthusiast, with no practical knowledge of the business. The details of the operation rested on the broad shoulders of Alexander Majors. He bought new stock and vehicles and then set the line running on a regular schedule; soon he lengthened it to Salt Lake City.

Now at this time, while Congress was resolutely keeping its eyes shut to the Overland Trail—while the contract mail from St. Louis

to San Francisco was being hauled by the old
Butterfield Line via Texas, New Mexico and
Arizona—there was one man in Washington
who was almost fanatical in his determination
to force the recognition of the shorter mid-
land route. This was Senator W. M. Gwin of
California. In the winter of 1859–60 there re-
curred to him an idea which he had gotten
two years or more before. At that time he had
been journeying eastward from California
and had fallen in with Fen Ficklin, one of
Alexander Majors' superintendents. The two
had talked over the feasibility of a relay express of horsemen to carry letters across the
continent after the manner which old Jenghiz
Khan, the Tartar ruler, had used in Asia many
centuries before. With the recurrence of this
idea, Senator Gwin thought he saw a chance
to convince his fellow-legislators of the Overland Trail's feasibility as a mail route. Fate
so willed it that W. H. Russell of Russell,
Majors & Waddell met Senator Gwin in
New York at just this time. And before Gwin
and a number of associates got through with
Russell, the enthusiast had pledged his firm
to undertake the organization of a pony ex-

press line from Missouri River points to Sacramento, California.

Russell went back to Leavenworth, Kansas, and told his partners what he had done. When he finished talking, there was a dead silence for some moments. Then Alexander Majors declared quietly that if they did this thing they would lose a quarter of a million dollars.

But Russell had pledged his word, he said. With Majors a promise was apparently more sacred than a quarter of a million dollars; he withdrew his opposition and took on his wide back the enormous burden of the task which his partner had so blithely agreed upon. So, by the enthusiasm of one who did not know what he was really doing, and by the rigorous conscience of another, who realized all too well what the undertaking meant, the most picturesque act in this nation's drama of transportation came to be staged.

Now Alexander Majors went to work as he had never worked before. It was about the first of February, 1860; the line was to be in operation during the first week of April.

He chose the short route—the old emigrant

trail up the North Platte and the Sweetwater, by way of Fort Bridger to Salt Lake; thence on to California. Along the eastern end, as far as old Julesburg, near where the North and South Platte join, there were already many established change stations for the stage line and for the freighting business. With these as a foundation, Majors established a chain of stations, on the average of less than fifteen miles apart, from St. Joseph to Salt Lake City; he stocked them with feed and hay; he bought saddle horses and he hired riders. On the west end, from Salt Lake City to Sacramento, California, Bolivar Roberts built a line of these stopping-places through the wilderness. You can see some of those buildings yet along the Lincoln Highway between Austin and Carson City, Nevada, with their thick walls of cobblestones or adobe, and the narrow loopholes for the rifles of the hired hands when the Indians were trying to wipe them out.

There had been an unusually heavy snow-fall that winter and the drifts were nearly thirty feet deep at the summit of the Sierras. Roberts got a crew of men to work at beating down a trail for about fifty miles in the mountains. On the Carson Sink he got another crew to cutting willows and laying them corduroy fashion through the worst part of the mud.

It was after the first of February when the work was begun. By the first of April the line was ready for operation. Every fifteen miles—and in heavy going the interval was less—there was a swing station for the change of horses. Every sixty to eighty miles there was a larger station, with bunks and eating accommodations, where the riders changed. These distances were, in some cases, exceeded during the first few weeks of the mail carrying. The length of the route was 1,966 miles. There were in all one hundred and ninety stations, several hundred horses, eighty seasoned riders, and something like three hundred station-keepers and stock-tenders.

This line of men and horses and buildings stretched nearly two thousand miles. Most of that interval was wilderness. It included several snow-capped mountain ranges and long stretches of savage desert. It was peopled by the most warlike Indians in all the West. But in two months' time this man Majors had spanned it.

It was on the riders that this project now depended. Majors and Bolivar Roberts knew horses and horsemen; while they were buying good stock, they took care to hire men who could stand long hours in the saddle at a grueling pace—lean men, light of weight, and blest with that quality which was known as "sand." Majors insisted that every hand sign a paper promising not to swear or drink while he was on duty. That the messengers of the pony express held to the letter of this pledge is—to put it mildly—unlikely; but the rigidity of the requirement resulted in the weeding out of the drunken and loud-mouthed right at the beginning.

Their equipment was peculiar—for weapons a six-shooter and a bowie-knife; that was all, for steel weighs heavily, and speed was the whole basis of the idea on which the pony express rested. Rather flight than fight was the rule. Saddles and other harness were as light as possible. Over the saddle was a sort of leather covering which contained the pouches holding the mail. When the incoming rider leaped from his horse at a station, this covering was lifted off and placed on the waiting horse.

As to costume, the messengers for the most part had been working with the wagon trains or the stage lines; in their new calling they clung pretty much to their old raiment, save that they made it lighter. The double-breasted flannel shirt was frequent; often a rider wore a buckskin jacket. The limp-brimmed, wide felt hat with the low crown was almost universal, save in cold weather. The men looked much like the cowboys of the seventies and the eighties who were to follow them.

When the long shrill yell of the incoming rider reached a change station the relief messenger hurried outside; here the stock-tender had a fresh pony, saddled and waiting. The rider dashed in, stopped his horse and, as he leaped off, the station-keeper lifted the pouches from one saddle to the other. With the completion of this change—which was accomplished in a single brief movement of the arm—the relief messenger swung to the fresh pony's back and was off. Uphill and down, good trail and bad, he kept to a dead run. Only on the long grades did he let the pace slacken. Ten or fifteen miles, and then he saw the next swing station ahead of him. He uttered the long-drawn coyote yell; and

when he rode in he found a waiting pony.
The pouches were changed; he leaped to the
back of the new mount and was off again—
so from one swing station to the other for
sixty to eighty miles, and then a new messenger
took the pouches on. That was the method of
operation.

On April 3, 1860, the first riders started
from the eastern and the western ends. From
Sacramento, across the snow-covered Sierras,
to the sink of the Carson—one hundred and
eighty-five miles—took fifteen hours and
twenty minutes. The entire distance of 1,966
miles was covered by east and west going
pouches in ten days. Within a few weeks the
time was reduced to eight days, and the
weekly service became semi-weekly.

One of the most important news despatches
to go through was the tidings of Lincoln's
election. It took a little less than eight days
to bring it from St. Joseph, Missouri, to Sacramento, California. Pony Bob Haslam carried the pouches one hundred and twenty
miles through western Nevada in eight hours
and ten minutes—and took time for a running
fight with a bunch of Piute Indians who had
ambushed him near Sand Springs. During

the battle he got an arrow through the lower jaw which knocked out five of his teeth. Lincoln's inaugural address went through in just seven days; the news of the firing on Fort Sumter took eight days.

Most famous of the rides is that of Pony Bob Haslam. The Piute Indians were out when he started eastward from Virginia City. When he reached Reed's Station on the Carson River, sixty miles away, he found that the settlers had taken all the horses in their campaign against the savages. He fed the animal which he had ridden and pressed on to Fort Churchill, fifteen miles farther. Here the messenger who was to have relieved him refused to take the saddle, for fear of the Indians. Haslam mounted another pony, rode thirty miles to the sink of the Carson, got a change there, shoved on another thirty miles to Sand Springs, changed again, and continued by way of Cold Springs to Smith's Creek. There he turned the pouches over to J. G. Kelley. He had ridden one hundred and ninety miles. Nine hours' rest, and the westbound pouches came. Haslam started back over the route. At Cold Springs the Indians had massacred the station-keeper and stock-tender and run off the horses. Pony Bob spurred his jaded horse through the gathering night to Sand Springs, where he warned the station-keeper of the savages. On a fresh mount he raced to the sink of the Carson. From here on he found new horses at every station and finished his round trip of three hundred and eighty miles within a few hours of schedule time.

Even more grueling was the ride of William F. Cody, who was still in his teens. Cody started from Red Buttes Station on the Sweetwater in Wyoming one morning. His destination was the change station at Three Crossings. When he arrived at the latter point he found that the relief rider had gotten into a fight and been killed. So young Cody swung to the back of the fresh pony and rode on. One relay station after another; the leap from the spent horse, a bare moment on the earth, then the leap into the saddle on the fresh horse. So he went on, eighty-five miles to Rocky Ridge. He had rested here an hour when the rider from the east came in. Cody took the pouches and rode back over the same route—three hundred and twenty-two miles

—with only that hour's rest, and he arrived at Red Buttes on time.

During the operation of the pony express only one mail was lost and one rider killed; and this in spite of floods, of blizzards, and Indians on the warpath. Within a few months the line opened the stubborn eyes of those at Washington; they saw the thing which the people had discovered nearly thirty years before. Recognizing the practicability of the Overland Trail, they chose it for the route of the transcontinental telegraph. So, while the pony express was shortening the time between the two oceans, the poles were going up; the wires were being strung. In October, 1861, the messages were being flashed from San Francisco to Washington. And Alexander Majors took his ponies and his riders off the road. His firm had lost just two hundred thousand dollars.

In the meantime Russell, Majors & Waddell had extended their stage from Salt Lake City to Placerville, California. And, now that the telegraph attended to the rapid communication, they got the contract for carrying the mails.

At the beginning of the Civil War the Indians got word of what was going on. Already
many of the tribes were restless because of
the rapid extermination of the buffalo and the
building of the telegraph line, which latter
institution was regarded by the savages as
bad medicine. So now there came a general
outbreak, from Minnesota to the Sierras. And
the Overland Stage Line got the brunt of the
fighting.

Stations were burned; men were killed and
stock run off in Nevada, Wyoming, Colorado
and Nebraska. In the early autumn of 1862
the line went out of commission along the
Sweetwater for more than two weeks, after
two hundred Sioux had killed the driver and
two passengers in a running fight against the
east-bound stage between Split Rock and
Three Crossings. During this interim some
thirty-odd station-keepers and stock-tenders
were gathered at Sweetwater Bridge. Under
the leadership of young Bill Hickok, who
had but newly come to his sobriquet of Wild
Bill, these employees took the trail of the
Sioux marauders, who had just run off some
more of the company's horses. They followed
the tracks more than half-way across the Ter-

ritory to the Crazy Woman's Fork of Powder
River. There they found the Sioux village,
and Hickok bade them bide until dusk; then
he led them in a charge through the tepees.
They stampeded the stolen stock and the
ponies of the Sioux and brought them all
back, along with a number of dripping scalps
for souvenirs. In the three days' celebration
which followed their return to Sweetwater
Bridge, Slade, the famous bad man of old
Julesburg, slew one of his numerous enemies.

It was on the Overland Stage Line that
young William Hickok got his nickname of
Wild Bill, when he fought the six members
of the McCandless gang single-handed at
Plum Creek Station. Of that Homeric battle
much has been written elsewhere. Martha
Canary, better known as Calamity Jane, was
among the famous characters along the route
before she went to Deadwood.

They used six horses or mules to a coach.
The vehicle was an old-style thorough-brace
Concord. The time from Atchison, Kansas, to
Placerville, California, was seventeen days.
When the trail was level or downhill the ani-
mals were kept on the dead run for miles.
There were no bridges. The streams were

frequently swollen and the fords were often bad with quicksand. In winter blizzards were frequent enough to be called the rule rather than the exception. To keep to schedule under such conditions took drivers with rare nerve. But the mail was seldom late.

The stations were arranged very much as they had been on the pony express. The ordinary swing stations had only a keeper and a stock-tender. There were in addition to these the so-called home stations, where the coach made a long enough stop for the passengers to get a bite to eat. At these larger buildings, in many instances, the station-keepers had their wives and families. With the exception of the Mormons out in Utah, these were the first women settlers along the trail. And even in those years of danger and hardship they used to get occasional relaxation by riding forty or fifty miles to some station, there to dance until daybreak.

This Overland Stage Line had just got to working nicely and to making money when, through the folly of one member of the firm, it passed into the hands of Ben Holliday, the transportation magnate of that day. Alexander Majors found himself forced out of business.

For a few years he went back to freighting, and his long teams were seen on the rough old trail from Salt Lake City to the placer diggings about Virginia and Alder Gulch, Montana. And then there came a new change to the Overland highway. The Government had subsidized a transcontinental railroad by this route. From the west end men were building the Central Pacific; from the east end another group were building the Union Pacific.

Majors went to work for the latter as a subcontractor along the Bitter Creek section in southwestern Wyoming. Away back in his youth he had established the broadhorn record on the Santa Fé Trail. Now with the passing of the last of the old trails he established another record, which was not equaled by many subcontractors on that work. It is said of him that he never turned in a padded pay-roll. With the tying up of the rails at Promontory, Utah, rapid transportation—which Majors had begun with the pony express—became an established institution, henceforth to be taken for granted by a people who now find it hard to realize that there was once a time when the East and West were far apart.

CHARLES GOODNIGHT

WHEN the Civil War was over, Charles Goodnight rode home to the rolling jack-oak hills of Palo Pinto county. During the years between Fort Sumter and Appomattox he had been a Texas ranger, fighting the Comanches out on the Llano Estacado. Now he was penniless; his only assets were a herd of longhorns, depleted by thieves and by army levies, scattered by the northers of five winters.

Texas and he were very much alike. The two of them were going on thirty years of age—strapping, still full of fight. The war had given both a hard deal, but neither was discouraged. As they looked toward the future —lusty, ragged and eager-eyed—each saw the same material with which to build: a multitude of cattle and no one at hand to buy a pound of beef. The analogy becomes more intriguing when you realize that it hangs throughout the story. The tale of young Goodnight seeking his fortune becomes the chron-

227

icle of Texas rehabilitating herself. This, in its turn, becomes the chapter of the West which is best known as the cattle era—a splendid medieval period whose traditions will endure like those of European chivalry.

The animals on which the futures of Charles Goodnight and Texas hinged were not the cattle that we know to-day. Their ancestors had come from Spain with the conquistadores; they had crossed the Rio Grande from Mexico in the era of the old Spanish ranchos. After the Texan revolution, hard-riding young adventurers, many of whom had been orphaned by the Alamo and Goliad, harried the wild creatures out of the mesquite thickets and rounded them up in huge corrals, to slay them for the hides and tallow. By the beginning of the Civil War this cow-hunting had developed into cattle-raising, and a number of men owned fair-sized herds. With the struggle for secession these herds had once more lapsed to wildness. They roved the prairies and the brushy valleys, a leggy breed, small-bodied, shaggy, with enormous horns. A four-foot spread from tip to tip was not uncommon. They were as fleet as deer, as shy as antelope. From the Gulf coast to the southern edge of the Panhandle they grazed, along the western edge of the settlements. Bones, hide and horns made up most of their weight. But in their hard leanness—and in their ability to put on fat in regions where the blooded cattle of present herds would have starved— lay the virtue by which they were to make men's fortunes and to make western history. When it came to overland traveling, the camel of the desert was the only animal that rivaled them.

When Goodnight returned to Palo Pinto county he failed to see any opportunity in these scattered longhorns of his; so he turned his mind to other prospects. With three fellow-Texans who were in very much the same shape as himself he started for Old Mexico; but when they reached Devil's River, in the Big Bend country along the Rio Grande, Colonel C. C. Slaughter, who was one of the party, was accidentally wounded by a rifle. The rest gave up their trip to get him back to a surgeon. And at this time young Goodnight picked up the idea which meant so much for him and Texas.

Fort Sumner, New Mexico, was buying beef on the hoof from the Big Bend region.

This post on the upper Pecos River included a Navajo reservation, and that meant several thousand mouths to feed. Now the big young Texan saw possibilities in these four thousand longhorns of his. Six years before, he had trailed their fathers and mothers two hundred miles to their present pastures. He knew their ability to put on weight while they were traveling, provided they were properly handled. There was, he told himself, no reason why they could not make the six hundred miles to Fort Sumner in shape to pass the most rigid inspection.

To the average man—even the average Texan of those days—the route from Palo Pinto county to the upper Pecos country would have seemed impossible. When one departed from Fort Griffin he passed into a wilderness where enormous bison herds pastured; later on the water became scarce, finally to dwindle out entirely. There was an interval of more than ninety miles without a drop of moisture. Here, on the flat arid reaches of the Llano Estacado, the Comanches found their haven when pursuit from the settlements grew too hot for them. From the headwaters of the Brazos and the Concho, and all the way up the Pecos River, they claimed the land, and the white man who traveled through it must be prepared to fight if he hoped to keep his scalp.

Herein, however, the Civil War had done young Goodnight a good turn. For he had been putting in the past few years in this same land beyond the western settlements. The upper reaches of the Brazos and the Concho were familiar ground to him. He knew the Llano's every water-hole. Indian-fighting had become his trade; he could read a trail as well as any Comanche.

There was but one thing lacking for his project. To drive a herd meant hired hands and horses. And these, in their turn, meant money. The year of 1866 had passed before he found a partner with financial backing. Then he ran across Oliver Loving, an old-timer in the cow business and willing to take a chance. In the spring of 1867 the two of them started gathering their herd.

In those days men were far more plentiful than dollars throughout the State of Texas. So the hands began to make their appearance right away. If any one had called them cowboys then, they would not have understood the term. They were typical products of the times; and the times had trained them well for this wild calling. Some of them had been hardened in the powder smoke of Shiloh and other bloody fields. The others had grown up during the war in this neighborhood. Life hereabouts had been a rough proposition. With the Comanches raiding all along the border every light moon, these youths had learned to draw down their rifle sights while the arrows were buzzing around their ears. More than one of them had scalped his dead Indian. In all there were fifteen of them; seasoned riders, blessed with the coolness that makes a brave man worth his salt. Many of them wore boots, but the high heel of cattle-land was yet to come; their headgear ran to wide brims, the forefathers of those low-crowned Stetsons which were to be worn wherever cattle ranged. Every one of them brought along from one to four six-shooters and a well-oiled needle-gun or Enfield rifle, the latter slung under his stirrup leather.

In the weeks of late spring they hunted the wild longhorns out of the hills and jack-oak thickets, harrying them to the holding ground. They spent fervid hours in the stifling dust, breasting the surging, bawling packs to the long wings leading in to the branding-corrals.

Spring was drawing on toward summer when they took the trail; two thousand lowing cattle, with the lithe young riders flanking them, on point and swing and drag; a number of pack-mules laden with grub, bedding and supplies; and the *remuda* of seventy-odd ponies. Ahead of the long cavalcade young Goodnight rode, setting the pace for the lead cows. And as he rode he watched the earth ahead of him, reading the faint signs which it bore, translating them into the men or animals that had left them there.

Their course lay southwest from old Fort Griffin to the Horsehead Crossing; then up the Pecos to Fort Sumner: a roundabout way, but it was the only route where there was water. At first they traveled through limestone hills dotted with scrub-oaks. Wild game was plentiful; the bison herds were always in sight; and the Indians were doing their marauding somewhere else that season. So they went on, crossing the low divides between the headwaters of the Brazos and the Colorado; the Colorado and the Concho.

Unvaried by Indian fight or stampede, the

routine of the long days went on; twilight of early morning and a bite of breakfast by the little fire; sunrise and the slow departure of the herd from the bedground; the leisurely advance growing from grazing to a swinging, steady walk; the hours in the dust clouds and the rising heat; water and the return to grazing with the waning of the day; then the bedground, with the two night herders circling the mass of drowsing cattle from opposite directions, until their guard was done and they crept into their blankets among their sleeping companions, with the hard earth beneath them and the yellow stars overhead.

So they reached the last waters of the Concho, with the dry floor of the Llano Estacado ahead of them—ninety-two miles of level plain, without a landmark, without a waterhole. They held the cattle here late into the day, letting them drink, then drink again— and still again—until every animal had taken the last drop it could hold. At length they started out across the table-land.

When that night came, instead of bedding down, they kept right on. So they traveled through the hours of darkness, and when the dawn lifted it found the herd strung out, plodding slowly forward, the weary riders in the dust clouds hanging to its flanks. A long, long day; a longer night; another day whose hours were torture. The cattle barely moved; now and again they halted, gazing through the dust clouds with reddened eyes; and the red-eyed riders spurred their gaunted horses against them, urging them on with yells and waving coats, until they resumed their hesitant pace. Night came; the herd had become a straggling line stretched out along more than two miles of plain. The sun shot up; the heat grew; the dust clouds thickened. Now and again a rider reeled in his saddle, dead asleep; some moistened their eyelids with tobacco juice that the torture might keep them awake. Before them the land began to slope away into the twelve-mile canyon that led down to Horsehead Crossing. The heads of the riders were bowed; the horses stumbled, their flanks drawn in by thirst; the muzzles of the cattle touched the earth. Their low moaning rose, a never-ending plaint. When they halted, the men surged upon them firing their six-shooters to keep them moving. Some of the steers stood fast. The thirst had blinded them.

Then there came a little breeze. Two or three of the stronger animals in the lead raised their heads; their reddened nostrils widened as they sniffed the air. Their lowing took on a new note. They started forward at a steady walk. Others, hearing that new note, followed; and then their voices joined those of the leaders. Twelve miles to the river, but the scent of the water had reached them. They began to advance once more as a unit.

So they came, strung out over three miles, down to the Pecos. And the men worked till darkness stopped them, hauling bogged-down cattle from the quicksands under the bank.

That was the last of their ordeal. Their journey up the valley was without interruption; and when they reached Fort Sumner, Loving and Goodnight got eight cents a pound on the hoof for their longhorns.

The next year Loving and Goodnight met their first opposition from the Indians. The herd had been gathered from the valley of the Brazos and was being held near Fort Griffin. In the dark hour just before the breaking of the dawn the two riders on the last night guard were making their slow rounds; the others were sleeping in their blankets by the chuck wagon. A dozen saddle horses were tethered to a long picket rope close by; the *remuda,* of more than fifty ponies, was two or three hundred yards away. Out of the darkness came the thunder of hoofs; the shrill war yell of the Quahada Comanches. Arrows buzzed like huge wasps among the awakened men. Two hundred warriors were sweeping down upon them.

The cattle were on their feet. In the passing of the instant they were off, two thousand of them, packed so tightly that their long horns were clicking as they ran. The two night herders spurred their ponies, heading toward the point to turn them. They might as well have tried to turn a rain-swollen mountain river.

As Goodnight sprang from his blankets an arrow struck the flint hide buffalo robe on which he had been lying and glanced away beneath his body. "It's the *remuda* they are after," he called. With him half a dozen others rode on the dead run. And as they came, they caught glimpses of dark forms speeding through the grayness of the night

toward the band of horses. Then their rifles
and six-shooters spat thin streaks of flame.
The Comanches swerved off and the cowboys
dashed between them and the ponies.

Inside of half an hour the fight was over.
Having failed to drive off the *remuda,* the
Indians melted away into the twilight of the
approaching dawn.

Meantime the stampeded longhorns were
racing off across the plain. Several men had
reinforced the two night herders. In the darkness there was no chance to see the land or
guide a horse. They rode, reins loose, taking
the footing as their mounts found it; gully
and cut bank, boulders and brush, with the
thunder of the cattle in their ears and the
black mass of bodies close upon them, frothed
with the gleaming horns. Now the mass began
dividing. A rider stayed with every bunch.
The light grew stronger, they pressed their
ponies against the leaders, yelling, firing their
six-shooters. The wearied animals yielded a
little, then a little more, until they were all
milling. So the segregated elements were
headed off, one after another.

Three hundred cattle were lost that night.
And the others were restive, ready to run at

the stirring of a reed in the breeze, at the appearance of a shadow.

On Elm Creek near the headwaters of the Clear Fork of the Brazos, the Comanches made another attack a week or so later. It was the hour before daylight when two or three hundred of the Quahadas came whooping through the darkness. The herd were on their feet and running before the cowboys in the chuck wagon were fairly awake. This time the battle for the *remuda* was more stubborn than before; the Indians made two or three charges from the shelter of a gully and were finally driven out with the approach of dawn. It took nearly all the day to round up the scattered cattle; some of the longhorns had run fifteen miles. So before they struck out across the Llano on the long dry drive, the losses had already swelled to four hundred.

Two weeks later, when the herd was nearing Fort Sumner, Oliver Loving set out ahead with the idea of riding on to the post and arranging for a figure with the government beef-buyers. Young Goodnight had found Indian signs that day; so the older cattle man took with him a companion, J. M. Wilson, a one-armed veteran of the Confederate army.. It was a long day's ride. The two pressed on as fast as possible.

Along toward noon they forded the river and came up out of the timbered bottom-land and to the open mesa. Soon afterward they got sight of some Comanches ahead of them. They turned and raced back toward the stream. Now six hundred Indians, bare bodied, streaked with war paint, came yelling after them. The horses of the white men were already jaded from the journey. The savages were on fresh mounts. The distance between pursuers and pursued was narrowing rapidly. When the river was still a hundred yards away, Loving and Wilson leaped from their saddles and took to cover in a little nook which the rains had gullied out of the steep bluff. The former was bleeding from two wounds. The Indians swept toward them in a dense mass; but the charge broke before the deadliness of the two rifles. Then Wilson helped Loving pull an arrow from his side.

Another charge; and after that the savages settled down to make a siege of it. Loving felt his strength was going.

"You swim the river," he told Wilson, "and I'll stand them off from here. Perhaps you can get back to camp." Wilson demurred; but the older man insisted, and at last he went. What with his clothes and his rifle, and with the swiftness of the current swollen by some recent rains up in the mountains, he was unable to make the crossing. So he stripped himself and struck out, naked, without a weapon.

In the meantime Loving's horse had swum the stream and galloped back to the herd. When they saw the blood upon the saddle, Goodnight and a couple of cowboys took the back trail and followed it until darkness halted them. The next morning, just as they cut the trail of the six hundred Comanches, they got sight of a strange figure coming toward them. It was Wilson, stark naked, half-crazed from thirst and from exposure. They hurried on to the spot where he had left Loving.

Loving had held off the Comanches until night, and they had left in the darkness. A passing wagon outfit, fording the stream near-by, had discovered him soon after sunrise and

taken him on to Fort Sumner. Here Goodnight found him, dying from gangrene and
loss of blood.

So the Goodnight trail was beaten down in
blood and dust; and now other drovers began
to take advantage of the first outlet to a waiting market. With the competition, prices
dropped at Fort Sumner. Young Goodnight
moved his cattle on to Colorado and pros-
pered for two years; then a bank failure swept
away his new-found fortune. And when he
looked about him for an opportunity to begin
all over again—he found it back in Texas,
created by the conditions which he himself
had done so much toward establishing.

During these last years of the sixties Texas
had awakened to the opportunity which he
had proved. And, as the value of her longhorns began to show, there came new outlets
to other, larger markets. Jesse Chisholm had
made a trail for freighters' outfits across the
eastern portion of the Indian Territory—
which is now Oklahoma—and before 1870
a dozen drovers had driven herds over this
route into southeastern Kansas. Now Coffee-
ville and Abilene and Wichita became the
objective for multitudes of longhorns. And

now Dodge City appeared as a shipping-point to the Chicago stock-yards. The western trail was beaten down by myriads of cattle, some of them from beyond the Rio Grande. Then the Indian reservations of the two Dakotas and Montana came into the market as buyers; and the long trails went on northward to the Canadian boundary. Occasionally a drover, finding poor prices, held his cattle over winter and discovered that they put on great weight in these northern ranges. So the first ranches in Wyoming and Montana came into being. And the Texas drawl began to spread over all the lands of free grass, along with the thirty-foot grass rope and the double-cinch saddle.

Where the long trails ended at the shipping pens the cow-towns gave the cowboys relaxation after weary weeks in the saddle. In all the history of hazardous callings, where rough men lived always close to death, there is to be found no other breed as clean of heart and as decent of behavior as these young rowdies of the saddle. But when they came to the railroad, to mingle with the cold-eyed riffraff who were biding there to plunder them; when they drank the corroding whisky and were beset by the painted women of the dance-halls—the most of them, to use their own term, "cut loose." So there came into being, in all these cow-towns, that breed of heavily armed peace officers who have gone down in tradition as gunmen. A few of these, like Wild Bill Hickok and Bat Masterson, were men of parts and of repressions. Others who gained fame were calculating murderers. And none of them are to be confounded with the brave type of frontier sheriff who helped to bring the law into the more remote communities. In Dodge City and Ogallalla and Wichita there passed brief intervals— usually two years and sometimes three—when six-shooters blazed sometimes by night and men died with their boots on. Then the law was more quietly administered.

So the cattle days passed and the cowboy traveled on the long trails from north to south, cutting the older trails of the trappers, the freighters, the emigrants and the prospectors. And the range was dotted with the herds. The open country was ready for the farmer.

All of this came out of Texas. And, with its coming, Texas began to prosper. And when Charles Goodnight found himself ruined in Colorado he turned his eyes to his native State. He saw the lands of the free grass in the Panhandle, where the buffalo had been thick a few years before. He trekked back to the Canadian and started in anew at raising cattle not far from where the town of Amarillo now stands. He was just in time to take advantage of the rising market at Dodge City. In a few years he was richer than he had ever been before.